MW00473121

The Life of Father Aloysius

Second Edition

Fr. Charles Thomas Carpenter, M.A.P.

With ecclesiastical permission

Copyright © 2019 by Charles Thomas Carpenter
All rights reserved. No part of this book may be reproduced or transmitted through any form nor by any means, electronic or mechanical, which includes photocopying and recording, nor by any system of storing or recuperating information, without the written permission of the author.
Cover photograph, courtesy of Jerry and Janet Pevehouse Studios:
Father Aloysius Ellacuria, CMF, blessing author in 1975.

This book is dedicated with deep gratitude to our Founder,
Father Aloysius Ellacuria CMF (†1981),
who by his life of love taught others to know God.

N. B. In obedience to the decrees of Urban VIII, of March 3, 1625, and June 16, 1631, and to other similar Pontifical legislation, the author declares that no other credence is to be given to the contents of this volume than that given to human authority, especially in relation to supernatural gifts and graces where the Church has not intervened by her judgment. The author declares, moreover, that in no way is it intended to anticipate the decision of the supreme Ecclesiastical Authority.

*"It is a greater work to make a just man out of a sinner,
than to create heaven and earth."*

(ST. AUGUSTINE)

Preface to Second Edition

FIFTY YEARS HAVE PASSED since I met Father Aloysius in 1969, and I have already celebrated my fortieth anniversary of the priesthood. With the passage of time, my gratitude has continually increased to Almighty God for the graces received through knowing Fr. Aloysius. He was the most excellent orientation for my priestly and religious life.

Almost twenty years have passed since the first edition of this book. The first edition ran out last year, so the moment has come for a new and improved edition. Improvements include updating the history of Father Aloysius's little Congregation in Mexico and the progress of his cause for sainthood. Likewise, new facts I've learned as well as a new perspective attained over the years have helped me repair other inaccuracies.

Previous to the first edition (2001), three other works on Father Aloysius had already appeared. After that time, three more works came into existence, one of them a wonderful movie, "The Angel of Biscay," that is often shown on EWTN, and is available on line and at Catholic bookstores. Although much of their content is the same, their differences provide an enriching complementarity.

On March 5–6, 2018, I was summoned to appear at the Archdiocesan Tribunal of Los Angeles. There I gave an official deposition, which took a total of six and a half hours. What I learned above all is how much holier our Servant of God is than I had previously imagined. This realization came through the hundreds of questions one is asked during the interrogation. When all fifty or so persons' depositions are finished, the whole packet will be sent to the Vatican.

When hearing these fine-tooth questions, many times I thought, *How difficult it is to be declared a Saint!* There's an old saying: "Only the saint is guilty until proven innocent." All of the questions, most of which were about the practice of virtue to a heroic degree, make it clear how sanctity involves a lot of suffering willingly accepted.

Yesterday a woman asked me, "Why does God want us to suffer so much just to do His Will?" No matter what I said, she did not seem fully persuaded. Afterwards, I recalled a saying by Leon Bloy (†1917), a holy philosopher who greatly contributed to the conversions of Jacques and Raïssa Maritain. Bloy said: "There are places in the heart that do not yet exist; suffering has to enter in for them to come to be." So, the questions that are asked in the depositions for the causes of saints show us there are multiple signposts and hurdles on the road to holiness, many of which involve pain. It is nothing more than another ascent to Calvary, so that each one can become the saint God wants you to be. By allowing pain, God is not "harming" us. Rather, He is liberating us from ourselves so that we can attain true happiness. It is one of the ironies about sanctity that, even if complete happiness is reserved to the next life, the saint, no matter what he or she suffers, enjoys the deepest peace of heart. No worldly happiness can attract a holy person to abandon this peace of soul that goes beyond all understanding. The "place in the heart that comes to be," is charity, which in the end is all that matters.

INTRODUCTION

This little book is my personal testimony about a great missionary of our times, Father Aloysius Ellacuria, C.M.F. Since I met him eleven years before his death, this work, called a "life," centers on the final years (1969-81), while making brief sketches of, or mere allusions to, the earlier years. The final period of his life coincides in general with the foundation of our order, the Missionaries of Fatima, to which Father Aloysius devoted all his remaining energy.[1] In founding our order, he affirmed his purpose was to save souls—*all souls until the end of time!*—and "saving souls" meant "making saints."

Father Aloysius taught that only one feature separates us from the Saints—*their faith*. Faith alone makes all the difference in the world. Neither defects nor sins have a right to hold us back from scaling the heights. The Saints were as human as we are, and sometimes possessed even greater moral and physical disadvantages than you or I. But disadvantages present challenges for God. We might say His favorite sport is to make Saints out of sinners. And the bigger the challenge, the more glory for God, when at the gallery of the Last Judgment, His masterpieces contrast with the poor raw material He started out with.

---

[1] The primary name of the Institute is: Missionaries of Perpetual Adoration (of the Most Blessed Sacrament and Perpetual Veneration of the Immaculate Heart of Mary). However, for civil effects we use our popular name—"Missionaries of Fatima." This is also appropriate because we were founded in Fatima, Portugal.

1

Such a life of faith, whether it is hidden or made public, eventually creates surprises. If it is hidden, God may wish to make it public. While it remains hidden, its secrets will first surprise the hidden saint, as we see in the autobiography of St. Thérèse of the Child Jesus. Sanctity, as St. Thérèse puts it, consists *not* in doing extraordinary things, but in doing ordinary things extraordinarily well, meaning with lots of love. This takes the insight that faith gives us. G.K. Chesterton, a great master of paradox, perceived that ordinary things are not only "more valuable than extraordinary things," but that "they are more extraordinary."[2] This is similar to, but raises one beyond, the natural awe both the metaphysician and the poet experience, for whom, "the highest state to which humanity can aspire is wonder" (Goethe).

Chesterton's paradox may help explain Father Aloysius's opinion about his own life. Once, when I suggested he write the story of his life, it was as though I had approached an ammonia-soaked handkerchief to his nose. Looking horrified, he cried, "There is nothing in my life worth writing about!"

Humility is sufficient to explain this utter refusal. Anyone who has not passed through a dark night of the soul cannot understand this. A necessary part of sanctity is the conviction of one's own misery. St. Bernard said, "Until you start smelling yourself like a dead dog, you are not holy." All the Saints experienced this state of repugnance. At some point in their lives they descended into "the hell of self-

---

[2] *Orthodoxy* (Garden City, NY: Image Books, 1959) p. 46.

knowledge." A few examples among many can be seen in the letters to their spiritual directors by such Saints as Padre Pio and Mother Teresa of Calcutta. When these letters were made public the secular reaction was of shock and disapproval.[3]

Humility, albeit at home with the ordinary, is the only source of magnanimity (greatness of soul). Father Aloysius had the magnanimity to attempt extraordinary things. So, the spectacle of his own life, in hindsight, with its audacious acts motivated by a simple faith, must have appalled him, as it did many others, when these events actually took place. On countless occasions, I remember quivering in doubt when he, to comfort others, would proclaim with absolute certitude what he saw to be the Will of God. This does not mean he was always right at every step of the way. Nonetheless, at least in the case of healings, no matter how unpromising a diagnosis seemed, time would prove him right. He was willing to take the humiliation of being wrong in some other matters. But

---

[3] Auguste Poulain, in his great book, *The Graces of Interior Prayer*, describes this state: "When the divine light is very vivid, we can no longer try to deceive ourselves. Such or such an act in our lives astounds us, so great is the malice or the folly that we see in it. If memories of this nature are intense and frequent, it is a true torment, a slight image of one of those that overwhelm the lost; their life lies open to them like some vast picture; they see the disorder of all their actions, and the spectacle is a source of horror to them.... This disgust is accompanied by a sentiment of confusion; we shall all experience it at the hour of judgment.... When the soul is really humble, this spectacle is at once a suffering and a joy" (pp. 113-14).

when it came to healing, there was never a doubt in his mind.

The controversial side of such a life must exist. Controversy, to some measure, has always surrounded a holy man or woman. What they say or do often jars us—we who trod the beaten path—as opposed to common sense. Those who are not prepared for the holy anomalies in life more readily fall victim to misunderstanding others.[4] Why?—The difference between the way God thinks and the way man thinks is as great as the difference between heaven and earth (Is. 55:9). And saints, even while on earth, are already with God (Eph. 2:6; Col. 2:12).

Underneath the painful controversies, I discovered a very simple human being who fearlessly imposed his hands

---

[4] Jacques Maritain, to describe this disconcerting aspect of the saints, says: "The saints always amaze us. Their virtues are freer than those of a merely virtuous man. Now and again, in circumstances outwardly alike, they act quite differently from the way in which a merely virtuous man acts... This is why there would be no saintliness in the world if all excess and all reason judges insensate were removed from the world" (*Existence and the Existent,* [New York: Vintage Books, 1966], pp. 55–56). G.K. Chesterton expresses the same dilemma another way: "The saint is a medicine because he is an antidote. Indeed that is why the saint is often a martyr; he is mistaken for a poison because he is an antidote. He will generally be found restoring the world to sanity by exaggerating whatever the world neglects, which is by no means always the same element in every age. Yet each generation seeks its saint by instinct; and he is not what the people want, but rather what the people need... Therefore it is the paradox of history that each generation is converted by the saint who contradicts it the most" (*St. Thomas Aquinas* [Garden City, NY: Image Books, 1956], pp. 23–24).

on the heads of suffering persons and accepted the consequences—sometimes negative—that this gesture often
drew upon him.[5] He considered this gesture and anything
else that may have drawn attention to be simply a part of
normal priestly ministry. To anyone who manifested
surprise, he would point out Our Lord's numerous
injunctions to his Apostles to heal the sick, raise the dead,
cast out demons etc.

THE FOLLOWING PERSONAL EXPRESSION, written from deep
gratitude to the man who best prepared me for the fifty
years which have since elapsed, may in some small way help
my religious community know the spirit of our Father
Founder. I have tried to be as objective as possible, but not
to the point of renouncing all subjectivity. That would mean,
I think, to renounce love.[6]

---

[5] Fr. Aloysius believed he had been "exiled" from Los Angeles for six
years (1963 to 1969) for blessing people while imposing his hands on
their heads or, at least, from the attention this kind of prayer drew. In
regard to contrariety, Father Aloysius liked to remind us that St.
Anthony Mary Claret was "one of the most slandered saints of all times."
This he considered normal, according to the Eighth Beatitude. In her
biography of St. Teresa of Avila, Marcelle Auclair sees the calumnies
surrounding St. Teresa and St. John of the Cross to be so great and so
many, that it still is impossible to unravel them satisfactorily (*Teresa of
Avila* [Garden City, NY: Image Books, 1959], pp. 339–60).
[6] A great theologian stated: "Genuine objectivity is the fruit of authentic
subjectivity. It is to be attained only by attaining authentic subjectivity"
(Bernard Lonergan, *Method in Theology* [New York: Herder and Herder,
1972], p. 292). After asserting that "our authenticity consists... in self-
transcending... in true love," (ibid., 117), it is easier to realize why, for
Lonergan, "God is not an object" (ibid., 341-42). It took me twenty years
to start writing this book. The Gospels were not written immediately

after the death of Christ. When I learned this in New Testament studies, I wondered if the inspired writers needed several years to sort out what they knew about Christ from what arose from their personal reactions to Him.

I.

First Encounter

T he unforgettable day I met Father Aloysius Ellacuria, C.M.F., was November 7, 1969, at St. Michael's Church in Los Angeles. I was 24 and the occasion was the recitation of the rosary for my granduncles, Thomas and Lewis Nash, whom my father, on the morning of November 3, 1969, had found murdered in their own living room. From the large blood stains on the floor and walls, it appeared a horrifying struggle at self-defense had taken place the evening before. These old-timers had been stoned and then stabbed repeatedly by two teenage hoodlums.[1]

From the moment of this tragic event, all and within one week, five unusual circumstances seemed to serve as "steps" for me toward God. I will not enlarge upon them, but today they convince me that God had arranged everything for the decisive step, which was my encounter with Father Aloysius.

I prepared to attend the rosary for my granduncles by going to confession the previous evening. When I

---

[1] Thomas (age 92) and Lewis (age 89) lived in a small, deteriorated wooden house in a very dangerous area. The police afterwards informed us they had to tackle 80 criminal cases in one square mile of the neighborhood on that (Halloween) weekend alone. The butcher knives were taken from the kitchen. The stones were mining samples my granduncles had brought back from Prescott, Arizona. They used to say that if they ever found gold they would give every bit of it to the Church.

stepped out of the confessional, it seemed as though the lights in a dark room had suddenly been switched on. From that moment, I, who had never understood the common expression about "seeing God in his creation," began to see the hand of God literally in *all* day-to-day occurrences. But what happened the very next day, at the rosary, was to light up my path for good.

This is how it happened. Following the recitation of the rosary, everyone passed by the caskets to take leave of their two elderly friends. The church was packed. Contrary to custom, the caskets remained firmly bolted; the wounds would have repelled the most callous among us. As we passed up center aisle the funeral director, just behind me in line, whispered, "Did you know Father Aloysius is here?"

"Who Is Father Aloysius?" I asked.

"You don't know Father Aloysius!" he gasped.

The name did not sound entirely unfamiliar. My granduncles used to tell the children among us the more exciting stories taken from Father Aloysius's sermons. And somewhere in my memory was a fleeting visit my family had made to see him when I was only twelve years old.

The funeral director's face beamed as he lowered his voice: "He's that famous Spanish priest! And he's right there in the back of the church."[2]

---

[2] Several months later, I learned the cause of the funeral director's (Mr. McGlynn) special endearment to Father Aloysius. Years before, his wife had been completely healed of cancer through Father's blessing.

Passing the caskets, I followed the others to the left aisle of the church where I found my father. I told him what I had just heard, adding I did not know who Father Aloysius was. Amazed by my ignorance, my father insisted I meet this priest. He led me through the crowd to the back doors. We saw Father Aloysius on the sidewalk, taking leave of clinging admirers. My father greeted the priest and introduced me to him.

The physical presence of this priest alone had a profound effect on everyone. There is a certain light that shines from devout souls, to which St. Paul refers when speaking about Moses who used to hide his face with a veil so that the light would not be perceived (2 Cor. 3:13).[3] Regarding this light, I have always assumed it was spiritual, and not something physically perceptible.[4] In my first

---

[3] St. Paul further explains: "All of us, gazing on the Lord's glory with unveiled faces, are being transformed from glory to glory into his very image by the Lord who is the Spirit" (2 Cor. 3:18).

[4] Whether it was more than spiritually detectable did not concern me until one day in 1988, seven years after the death of Father Aloysius, I was passing through Phoenix, Arizona. On a routine pastoral matter, I called a priest completely unknown to me, who asked me to identify myself. In so doing, I came to explain my work, and mentioned Father Aloysius. The priest, whose name I no longer recall, became elated and told me it was precisely Father Aloysius who had told him when he was a little boy to enter the seminary. Our conversation then centered around Father Aloysius and eventually the question of the "light" came up. Thrilled, the priest from Phoenix went on to say: "For me it was more than a spiritual light, it was actually *physical*. One time I walked into a huge meeting hall where all the priests of the Diocese were assembled. My eyes immediately singled out Father Aloysius. He was seated at a

encounter with Father Aloysius, even though this luminosity played a part in the overall impression, what really overwhelmed me was something inside me that seemed to cry: "Finally, this is the man, right here in front of you, who can answer all your questions!" This conviction could not come from the merely physical. Facing me was an old priest dressed in a black cassock topped by a thin white surplus. But, at that moment an image engraved itself on my soul.

Father Aloysius was then promptly whisked home by his dutiful driver. My heart followed him to the other side of the sprawling metropolis where I imagined him to pass his days recollected in some monastery turret, inaccessible and incomprehensible to the surrounding *saeculum* with its bright lights and hectic lifestyle. I was not one for tracking down a priest, and I felt the great spiritual gulf separating us... Our next contact remained a secret of God's mercy.

Immediately I started going to daily Mass in the nearest church (St. Joseph's in Hawthorne) which, I found out later, was where I had been baptized. Everything now seemed to rest perfectly in God's hands, so I was not looking forward for anything better to take place. But, one morning an elderly Irish gentleman approached me in the back pews. He identified himself as a close friend of my deceased

---

table, and there was that light shining from his face! I walked up to greet him. He recognized me at once. After so many years of my not seeing him, how could he even remember my name? He said to me, 'I know you. When you were a little boy I told you you were called to be a priest.' So many years had passed since I was a child, but he had never forgotten me!"

granduncles, and explained how together they used to attend Father Aloysius's First Saturday Mass at the Claretian Missionaries.[5] He asked me if I wished to accompany him next time to that Mass. I leapt at the opportunity.

The much-awaited Saturday, December 6, dawned and, at 9:00 a.m., an old black Cadillac pulled up at the curb. In a half hour we were at 1119 Westchester Place, the new residence of the Claretians, built in the Spanish colonial style. The chapel is hexagonal, and its large arched windows invite one from inside to raise the mind to God from the artistically arranged gardens that carpet the cloister patio.

The Mass started at 10:00 a.m. The serene devotion with which it was celebrated left everyone deeply moved. I hung onto every detail as though I had never before attended a Mass in my life! It was literally conformed to St. Alphonsus's words often found over sacristy doors leading to the altar: "Priest of God—Celebrate this Mass as though it were your *first* Mass, as though it were your *only* Mass, and as though it were your *last* Mass." Had time itself stopped? Did everyone wish to remain in that sacred spell forever? The priest, with great unction and angelic gentleness, appeared to be *living* with his entire body and soul what he was saying. Every word of the Eucharistic prayer, even while pronounced with gentle restraint, was charged with heavenly power! The priest appeared in love

---

[5] This residence was built in 1968. A few years ago it was sold to a community of nuns.

with these words, as if their pronunciation alone were bringing delightful rapture to himself and to those who were fortunate enough to hear them.[6]

After Mass the elderly gentleman (my Irish Ananias) instructed me to wait in the corridor leading from the chapel into the lounge. Father would be passing by and greeting those who had attended Mass. When Father passed, we exchanged a standard greeting. My elderly friend immediately came to ask me what had taken place. I was so grateful to have received a personal greeting. He insisted, "What did he say to you?" When I repeated that it was a polite greeting, he urged me to approach Father once again because *something else* was supposed to happen. Seeing there were so many people claiming Father's attention, I thought, Why bother this priest? I remained where I stood. My friend became more determined. With a knowing smile, he firmly escorted me forward and, at the first (nearly) polite opportunity, actually butted in: "Father, this young man is the grandnephew of Tommy and Lewie Nash, members of our Guild!"[7]

---

[6] The Mass was celebrated in English. Although Father dearly loved the Latin language and was able to speak it fluently, the English language was no impediment for him to celebrate with the utmost devotion. He gave an exquisite example of how priests can celebrate without any excuses concerning the particular rite. He said that if the Church commands us to receive Holy Communion standing, we can receive it spiritually prostrate. He even mentioned that the new breviary in Basque was an overwhelming joy for him to pray with.

[7] The Guilds were made up of laypersons who met each First Saturday to pray the rosary and attend Mass with Father Aloysius. In very little

Father Aloysius's large blue eyes were incredibly expressive. Raising his eyebrows and riveting his attention upon me, he exhaled a long ascending "Oh-h-h-h?" First, he asked me if I knew electronics! When I answered "No," he asked me if I knew French. Enthusiastically I answered "Yes." In a very solemn tone, he responded, "I *need* you!"

These three words sank like welcomed pebbles to the bottom of a deep pond. Never before had I felt the thrill of being needed. At once, without any apparent cause, I, who knew of no personal future, began to *exist*. All of a sudden it seemed my life just might have some particular value. Father could do this with anybody. He discovered things within each of us, perhaps what we ourselves may never have imagined.

The throng surrounding Father then proceeded into a large hall off the lounge and I was invited to follow. Punch and finger sandwiches were being served. During this reception, which lasted an hour, Father Aloysius addressed the group on various spiritual matters concerning the First Saturday Guild of the Immaculate Heart of Mary. When finished, he suddenly spoke of the assassination of my granduncles who, being members of the same Guild, were known to most of those present. He explained their fate with great drama and pathos. After winding up the chilling account, he added that one of their relatives was seated at the back of the room and signaled for me to stand up.

---

time the number of guilds increased until there were at least five or six, each Guild scheduled for one day of the month.

From that moment I was accepted into the hearts of the Immaculate Heart of Mary Guild. To know Father Aloysius ordinarily meant to meet countless other persons whose lives were a powerful incentive to grow in faith. Later on in this book I will have occasion to give some of their personal testimonies in relation to Father Aloysius.

Immediately following the Guild meeting, Father Aloysius disclosed to me what purpose my knowledge of French would serve. In the following month, a nun from Paris, Soeur Marie-Joseph Bialgues, was to arrive in Los Angeles, and who would interpret? He confided to me that she was considered a "mystic" and would stay five weeks. My college French turned out barely sufficient, and by God's grace the poor nun managed to make herself understood by the hundreds of persons who flocked to consult her on various problems, both spiritual and material.[8]

---

[8] The visit of the French nun, Sr. Marie-Joseph Bialgues, was the first opportunity for me to get to know Father Aloysius better. Likewise, I learned something firsthand about extraordinary (charismatic) gifts. During the private interviews, I was astonished by her forthright answers to many widely different questions. Although I did not know the majority of the people who consulted her, most of them seemed overwhelmed by her deep perception. Once, I was allowed to verify for myself the validity of her remarks because a close relative of mine came to consult her. Although I had not told her anything about my family, she, without hesitancy, hit the stark truth in answering each question put to her. I believe it is to her credit that she was not educated. Upon entering anyone's house, she first would ask if they had a dog, because she loved to romp and frolic with these dogs. She had suffered very much during World War II with several other prisoners, locked up in the dungeon of the castle of Amiens. All were forced to drink their own

After Sister returned to her country, Father Aloysius invited me to continue living in the retreat section of the Provincial House. He needed plenty of help and, particularly in two areas: correspondence and driving.[9] I had recently arrived back from the Peace Corps, and I needed work. On the first task, I started by taking dictation (for personalized letters) and preparing standard replies (for donations arriving without enclosed messages). This involved stacks of letters every day. So much correspondence poured in that once a letter actually arrived without a street address. (The

---

urine, to eat nothing but one sardine every few days, and regularly to be placed blindfolded facing a firing squad while only one of them was shot. To this day I still recall the melody she and her companions used to sing before the firing squad.

[9] Father never learned to drive. He humbly considered himself "too nervous." Until October, 1971, I spent most of my time at the Claretian Provincial Residence. The Claretians invited me to live in the retreat section so that I could help Father Aloysius. After approximately one year, I saw myself as a "sponge," since I was provided with three meals a day and a place to sleep, all free. I told Father Aloysius I wanted to find a part-time job for the last eleven months. Father Aloysius said I did not need to do this, because the work as secretary and driver for him was already enough. But, because I thought I could handle both tasks I insisted. Plus, I knew we would have to help defray expenses for the upcoming novitiate in Fatima. So Father suggested I try out at Barone's Italian Restaurant on Riverside Drive in Toluca Lake, where Father's long-time good friend, Mr. Tony Arpaia, the owner, received me at the recommendation of Father Aloysius. I soon discovered this Restaurant was something of a 'training ground' for future seminarians and nuns, as I had occasion to run into other young people who also had been sent there by Father Aloysius before entering the religious life.

US post office already knew "Father Aloysius" in Los Angeles!) I was amazed by his superior command of English, his third language, which he had learned as an adult. He was very careful about how he expressed himself, and even had a refined way of pronouncing certain words: e.g., *incognito* and *exquisite* were stressed on the antepenult. Sometimes his dictation would fade in the middle of a sentence—he might be searching his memory for a more precise word, or attempting to clarify a grammatical construction, and, if I looked up, I might even find him asleep! (In the last case, I had a difficult decision to make: should I wake him up or let him get the needed sleep?...) For the next four years, typing letters alone usually occupied several hours each day.

The second task, driving Father around the city, came as a welcome break from the typewriter in my cell. Father visited the sick far and wide and frequently celebrated Mass at the Sisters Servants of Mary. These jaunts gave me the opportunity to meet a wide variety of persons of all social classes and in parts of the city hitherto unknown to me, a native. A few times I found myself in front of persons whose names I had seen or heard in the media. The drive especially gave me precious time to speak with Father.

I enjoyed the immense and undeserved privilege of living under the same roof with Father. It was as if I had found the bonfire to which burning embers along my trail had steadily been leading. Never before had I experienced that special feeling—always when I was around him—of being fully at one with God and the universe. Several times

I attempted to reveal to him everything of which I was conscious concerning my soul. To this day, I have never found anyone so capable of understanding the intricate and troubled depths of the human heart. Within the personal history of a soul, he would detect God's providence busily at work.

Those years, then, were marked by supreme happiness. In addition, Father, through his tactful care of souls and his incisive comments as we went along, manifested inestimable treasures about the priestly life. When I had the courage, I would ask him about his priestly history. He would answer with true humility, giving all the glory to God.

Looking back over fifty years, I thank our loving God for providing me with Father Aloysius. What a holy guide! Those years with him were so valuable, not only as a means to know a man considered by many to be a saint, but also to prepare me to understand the ideal life of the priesthood of Christ.

Father often explained that everyone's deepest motivation is to love and to be loved. His pastoral attention made people feel intensely loved by God. In this spirit he chose St. John the Evangelist, the beloved Apostle, as the model saint for his foundation of Missionaries of Fatima, because of the importance of being loved. One of the highest duties of fraternal charity is to liberate others so that they might become what God intends them to be. If it is true that man fulfills his greatest potential through loving, I would judge that Father Aloysius went further in this respect than anyone I have ever known. He spent his life enkindling this flame of love in everyone he met.

II.

Charisms and Holiness

During the year I remained at the Claretian Provincial Residence, the peaceful setting had its own jittery backdrop of calls alternating between the front door and the phone. Ninety percent of these calls, usually posed as "urgent," were for Father Aloysius. Thus, delicate battles were waged by the receptionist who, with the patience of a Titan, did her best to sift things out. Why all the commotion? Why were people looking for Father Aloysius?

Reactions to big favors are never easy to repress. Favor is stretched from little things, like sandwiches or fruit shakes made by his own hands for the hungry, to larger matters, like settling enmeshed family conflicts and, above all, healings. Healings became the primary attraction for most people. An excerpt from a letter by Bishop Juan Arzube sets the tone:

> Since I was aware of his gift of healing, I sent several persons to see him for that purpose. A few instances stand out in my mind.
>
> Mrs. Maria Rosa de Cuculon, originally from Ecuador but at the time residing in Los Angeles, California, called me to ask for my prayers. She had been diagnosed to have a cancerous tumor and was going to be hospitalized for an operation. I told her about Father Aloysius, and arranged for her to see him. He blessed her and told her she did not need an operation because she was healed, but added "If you wish to have the operation, please go ahead, but you don't need it." The lady went to see her doctor, and there was no evidence of the tumor. This happened over 25 years ago, and the tumor has never reappeared. Every time she sees me, she tells everyone about her miraculous cure, and thanks me profusely for having sent her to see Fr. Aloysius.

In the same letter, the Bishop adds: "Because of his kindness and miraculous cures, Fr. Aloysius had quite a following."[1]

Anyone who dedicates even a month to investigate the life of Father Aloysius, invariably finds precious testimonies where least expected. Jeff Moynihan in his book, *Wonder Worker in America*, states: "There were probably at least several hundred people cured by God through the priestly blessing and prayers of Father Aloysius (for over a period of 41 years)."[2] I do not question Jeff's assertion, since I have heard personal testimonies, as well as being present at the healings of several others. In fact, today, when I encounter anyone who personally knew Father, the conversation frequently swings to healings received either by oneself or among one's own family or friends. Mr. Francis Levy, several years after having written *Our Guide*, did further research on Father Aloysius. He writes:

> I began doing the things that one always dreams of doing in retirement... One fruitful enterprise for me was the succession of video interviews which I undertook to document the life of Father Aloysius. In this project I was able to tape the stories of fifty people who had known him and had experienced his many blessings... There is a lot of pertinent information available in these interviews... Some of them are quite lengthy.[3]

Before touching upon this more spectacular aspect of Father's apostolate, I would like to clarify, as briefly as

---

[1] Letter from Bishop Juan Arzube, Auxiliary Bishop of Los Angeles (retired), to Father Charles Carpenter, July 13, 1999.

[2] *Wonder Worker in America,* (Santa Barbara: Queenship Publishing, 1996) p. 4.

[3] Francis X. Levy, *Vestigia* (Alta Loma, CA: by the author, 2001), p. 161. See also *Our Guide* (Alta Loma: by the author, 1986).

possible, the concept of "charisms" according to official Church teaching. Charisms do not sanctify the person gifted with them, rather they are a "social" grace (i.e., for the good of others), given by God to build up the Church.[4] Charisms do tend to indicate holiness in a charismatic person.[5] However, while admitting this probability, it is best in concrete cases to leave final judgment to Church authority. Very ordinary persons may be gifted with extraordinary charisms, even from birth, yet still lack special leanings toward evangelical perfection.[6] God, who is generous in His gifts, does not calculate our merits, but wishes through charisms to help as many people as possible, in spite of the unworthiness of the instrument. Thus, one principle of spiritual theology seems clear: strictly speaking, charisms are independent of personal sanctity. This means that not all saints possessed extraordinary charisms nor are all persons with extraordinary charisms necessarily saints. As a consequence, what should interest us in the lives of the Saints are not the extraordinary charisms which they may possess, but their virtues. In fact, the church officially declares her saints only after proving beyond doubt that the candidate practiced virtue to a heroic degree. *No miracle worked before death counts as a proof of sanctity.*

---

[4] Vatican Council II, *Lumen Gentium*, 12.

[5] An extraordinary charism tends strongly to accredit the person who possesses it. Further factors, however, are needed to conclude that it is God who accredits the holiness of a particular individual because, in principal, charisms are not lost through mortal sin.

[6] I know of two women (now deceased), one whom I met, who were widely known for their healing power and were visited by travelers from foreign countries. In life, these women were very ordinary persons without aims of pursuing holiness or even of religious practice. Unquestionably both of these women had the gift of healing. Many similar cases in other areas of the world could be brought forth.

Having made these observations, I would like to deal with Father Aloysius's renown for extraordinary charisms. This is done not to feed the reader's curiosity, but to give glory to God who alone is the author of such favors as a means of extending the Kingdom of God. Presuming this distinction will be behind us by the end of this chapter, I will then move on to what I believe is far more interesting and more profitable for us to learn—Father's virtues.

Without mentioning his luminosity and odor of sanctity, extraordinary charisms in Father Aloysius's life may be assigned to three categories: (1) reading of souls; (2) healing of the sick; (3) levitation. Apart from these three gifts, there were other events, sometimes occurring daily, that may be lumped together in what the French call "meaningful coincidences in which God prefers to remain anonymous."

(I) **The gift of "reading souls"** nowadays is often called the gift of knowledge. Whether Father had this gift, and to what degree, calls for some clarification of the gift itself.

It may be recalled that Father hit wide of the mark when he asked me if I knew electronics. This fact however does not disprove the power to read souls when such a gift exists. God provides the faculty of reading souls to whomever he wishes, but usually to aid in giving spiritual counseling to others. Again, as a properly charismatic gift, "reading souls" is not a guarantee of personal holiness. Further, two conditions must be met before the gift of reading souls can operate. When they are not met, one is more likely to make mistakes.

(a) First of all, it must be God's will for something unknown in one's neighbor to come to light, at least to a confessor. Let us take an example. On one occasion, Sr. Marie Joseph Bialgues, of whom we spoke in the first chapter, told me before receiving a large group: "Tell them not to ask me what number wins the lottery!" Such questions are useless, for this kind of knowledge is not available to anyone. (God would have no purpose to reveal this.) Thus, any fact whose knowledge does not contribute to our salvation is ruled out.[7]

(b) The second condition is that the person who freely decides to approach a soul gifted with this special power should have the desire to be interiorly seen and understood. Without such a desire—at least implicit—a presumed power to see into another's soul becomes ineffectual, because God respects the intimacy of each soul. The soul is a sanctuary which God alone penetrates, with or without our consent. For God to permit others to violate this sanctuary would contradict a natural principle of ethics.[8] Exceptions are extremely rare, for example, in order to facilitate self-defense against willful infliction of grave harm.

Unless these necessary conditions are met, a person gifted with the interior power of reading souls simply will not perceive another's thoughts, no matter how holy the

---

[7] Fortunetellers, through satanic contacts, utilize their knowledge for lucrative purposes.

[8] This norm is not contradicted at the General Judgment. Most theologians believe all our thoughts will then be laid bare to everyone else. In the case of the saved, the Blessed will rejoice that others know their sinfulness, since God will thereby receive more glory for His infinite mercy (both at the sight of our sins and of our virtuous acts in doing God's will). In the case of the damned, their privacy will no longer deserve anyone's respect, and they will be acutely and eternally ashamed.

gifted person may be.[9] Even then, the gift is not always operative, and God will have His reasons.

In my own opinion, and allowing for the above conditions, Father Aloysius frequently utilized a special gift of reading souls. On various occasions, particularly in the confessional, he understood everything I knew about myself. One time, I remember him telling me the very words on my mind.[10] Countless were those who, when stepping out of the confessional, remarked: "I did not have to tell *him* what I did. He told *me* everything!" Those persons who came for spiritual counsel regularly left fully satisfied by his capacity to discern and resolve their difficulties.

Besides being able to "see" into the soul, he apparently obtained similar knowledge through a spiritual sense of smell. Sin, he told me, has a particular smell attached to it. Sometimes, especially in cases of impurity, the stench was nothing less than overwhelming to him. In spite of the fortitude he needed to sustain even a brief dialogue in these cases, Father was always filled with kindness toward all. (And, of course, he never did anything that might lead to identifying such persons.)

---

[9] St. Jean Vianney (Curé of Ars) had the gift of reading souls to an eminent degree. Nevertheless, he erroneously judged against the visionaries of La Sallette, while the Church later accepted their testimonies as worthy of belief.

[10] As an aside, I believe priests have this gift, at least to some degree, usually greater than they realize or would dare to implement. That it is not an entirely supernatural gift, but empowers the natural gifts, is supported by the following statement of an eminent spiritual master, when commenting on the holy Curé of Ars: "The saints by long experience in the direction of souls and by a profound knowledge of the spiritual life with its interior development, may have acquired in time unnatural sagacity in judging their fellow men" (Ignaz Watterott, *Guidance of Religious,* [St. Louis, MO: Herder Book Co., 1950] p. 77).

Since the capacity to spiritually perceive supposes an attitude of openness on the part of the person seeking an interview, it should surprise no one that on occasion even a very gifted person might be hoodwinked. In fact, during our two year assignment in Portugal, a man and a woman from England, both con artists, concocted a tall tale to get Father to entrust them with our meager resources. After a few days of dealing with them, they disappeared before we finally grasped their snarled intentions. Thank God, they were only able to make off with our cook's purse!

The use of the gift brought benefits to countless persons. I recall one at a "rosary picnic" at Dominquez Seminary in Compton.[11] Among those attending was a young couple on the point of divorce. Elder members of their family who had brought them along as an afterthought, asked Father Aloysius to pray for this collapsing marriage, and if possible, to speak with them. Father agreed and the fiery couple was hustled forward. From a short distance I watched how Father gently placed their hands together, spoke with them most tenderly and, as usual, with his eyes shut. A few days later, a letter arrived at Father's desk from the young wife. She described how, upon arriving home from the picnic, she was compelled to run into the back garden of her home, so emotionally overpowered was she by a sense of gratitude. She threw

---

[11] The "Rosary Groups," founded by Father Aloysius, met regularly but informally for praying the rosary in homes set aside for that purpose, on Thursdays at 7:30 PM. These groups began at the home of Mrs. Betty Gaffney in Lynwood and were open to all comers. They soon spread out to other areas of the metropolis. The "rosary picnic" was a yearly get-together for these groups, usually held on the grounds of Dominguez Seminary.

herself upon her knees weeping profusely over her former obstinacy, saying she received "the graces of a new life, pouring down like rain upon me." In her letter she thanked God from the bottom of her heart for the complete transformation of her marriage.

One member of our religious community, in his dealings with Father Aloysius, admitted to having a similar experience:

> About one year before Father died, I traveled from Alamos to Los Angeles to see him. My soul was in great turmoil, as I was passing through a very "dark night," and I was in dire need of advice. I could not explain this inner turmoil to anyone because I myself did not understand what was happening to me. When I saw Father, I only greeted him, when he at once began to counsel me. And his spiritual advice was perfectly suited to heal all my spiritual maladies, *instantly*. All this happened without my having had a chance to say one word concerning myself! I went back to Mexico a different person.

(II) **The gift of healing.** Similar to the gift of reading souls was Father's perception of the will of God for each individual during the exercise of the gift of healing. When he blessed anyone, he always seemed to know what was taking place. I asked him how and why he knew this. He confided to me that if the Will of God was to work a cure, he felt something like a force flowing through himself into the person before him. When the sick person was not to be healed, no such feeling accompanied the blessing. That is, nothing flowed outward, even though Father dearly wished for each person to be freed of his or her ailment.[12] He often

---

[12] A written statement presented to me by Eileen Ivers reads as follows: "Eileen Ivers, whose son Bill Jr. was seriously ill with an inoperable brain tumor in 1974, relates that Father Aloysius offered Holy Mass for

stressed that such favors solely depend on God, and warned others never to attribute any of them to himself. He referred to his role as "my most unworthy instrumentality." When asked about it, he stated that all priests have this gift, basing himself on Our Lord's frequent injunctions to heal the sick.[13]

This section exhibits a random sampling of thirteen favors received through Father's prayers. I have cut down my recital to those events which I myself verified either by being present at the occasion of a healing or through speaking and corresponding with the persons who were healed.

[1] I saw a thirty-five-year-old man kneel down to be blessed after a Saturday morning Guild Mass. He explained he had advanced cancer in his thorax and had been told by his doctor he had six months to live. He inhaled shallowly because of the pain involved in expanding the lungs against the rib cage. Father Aloysius blessed his chest and asked him to breathe deeply. The pain was gone! Father then asked him if he had any other ailment. The young man appeared to resist the question; perhaps he felt

---

the parents and their nine children at the Claretian Center. Then Father told Eileen that Bill Jr. would die, that God wanted him, but that he was a good holy young man, and that they would be able to pray to him when he reached Heaven. Bill Jr. died within a few weeks, but the family had received great consolation."

[13] This is found in several places in the Gospels. And it is not reserved to priests. In a letter from one of Father's friends, the writer states: "A lady friend asked me to bring Father to her as she was ill. He couldn't go, so he sent me in his place. When I told him that she wouldn't want *me*, he said 'If she won't accept you, she won't accept me.'" (Letter from Mrs. Alta Flocca to Fr. Charles Carpenter, March 18, 1982.)

embarrassed to ask for more healing. Father insisted, and the man replied that little particles of shrapnel still remained in the back of his eyes, lodged there from a grenade explosion in the Korean War. In spite of the operation he had undergone years before, which successfully removed the larger particles, the more minute particles were impossible to extract. Therefore, any increase of light pained his eyes and he always wore dark sunglasses even indoors. Father blessed his eyes and told him to walk over to the window and stare into the sunlight. No pain! Father told me and the other young men present to accompany this highly-favored man to a restaurant and eat well, "because when cancer is healed, the new cells are those of a newborn baby, and they need to be fed!" The man came back to the monthly Masses, and I was able to prove to myself by follow-up talks with him that his cures were genuine.

[2] One evening when I was acting as porter, a Mrs. Joy Trainor from Redondo Beach appeared at the door, supported on one side by her mother, and on the other side by her daughter. She was in great pain and had tears in her eyes. Father told me to usher them into the chapel, where I left them until Father went in to bless them. About half an hour later, I saw the same lady walk through the lounge, a big smile on her face, and with no one's help. After the door closed behind them, I asked Father what happened. He told me he had nothing to do with it. His words, to the best of my memory, were:

> They were kneeling in the chapel when I arrived. The lady was full of cancer [Father indicated by passing his own hand over his entire chest-abdomen]. I asked the woman if she had prayed to God for a miracle. She said "no." So I explained to her how Christ is the same, twenty centuries ago as today,

and that he is *right here* in front of us in the Blessed Sacrament. And since Christ healed the sick persons when He walked on this earth, He can do exactly the same now. "Do you believe this?" I asked her. She said "yes." So I said, "Let us kneel and make the station to the Blessed Sacrament." We started saying the six Our Fathers and Hail Marys. After two or three Our Fathers the lady nudged me and whispered, "Father, I don't think it is necessary to go on! I feel *so good* inside. I must be healed!" So we stood up, and I told her, "Give all thanks to Almighty God, who loves you so much!" After a prayer of thanksgiving, I added as she left the chapel, "Lest you will be fooled by your emotions, go and see your doctor and tell him to examine you."

At about 11:00 the next morning, the lady called the Provincial House and told Father Aloysius that the doctor had taken x-rays and found—to his total astonishment— that all the cancer had disappeared. The invaded cells were replaced by "the cells of a newborn baby."

[3] The following cure is taken directly from a letter (October 27, 1999), addressed to me by Mrs. Susan Muffaletto of Northridge, California, whom I first visited about forty-five years ago with Father Aloysius, and with whom I maintained contact for another twenty years. This woman had experienced terrible pain, day and night, for four years. Her doctor had diagnosed her with a herniated disc in her spinal column and advised her that an operation "might be successful," with 50% odds she would never walk again. She said, "The pain was terrible. I could not eat or sleep or walk properly. I can honestly tell you that I did most of my housework on my hands and knees. I could not stand upright." One day her mother and her sister brought her to attend Father Aloysius's Mass and receive the blessing afterwards. She writes:

I remember feeling so weak and hurting so much, that I wanted to lie down, but my sister and mother kept helping me to stay at the railing.

Finally, the priest came to me. I know he said something, but I can't remember what he said. All I remember is that I looked up into his face. His eyes were so beautiful! I thought, "He is an old man, but he has the eyes of an innocent child! How can this be?" I was so overcome by the spiritual beauty of his eyes that I could not speak, or think sensibly. I know I should've tried to communicate with him, but so help me, I was so dumbfounded by his eyes, I could not move, or speak.

Then he put a hand on each shoulder of my body; upon feeling his touch, a wave of warmth flowed from his hands down each side of my back, down, down my entire back! As it (the sensation) ebbed away, I realized, with a great sense of amazement, that the pain was entirely gone! To this day, whenever I recall this wonderful event, the enormity of it all, takes my breath away!

The pain never came back.

You must understand, I did not know anything about Father Aloysius; I had never heard of him before; I did not know what I was doing there, or what to expect. If anyone had told me before they took me there, I was not even able to remember any of it. I was like a child lost in the woods. The miracle that was bestowed on me came like a bolt out of the blue.

There is more to this: how I went to my doctor, his wonderment of my recovery (he and I both cried); how Father Aloysius came later to our home, and on his second visit, how he told me about certain things about my future. But I know you just need the facts about my healing.

Father Aloysius has answered many of my prayers to him, after his death I find him to be such a friend and so much comfort to me. I cannot get over the fact that he is still working so hard to help us, even after he has earned his heavenly reward. If he is doing this for me, surely he is helping others, is it not so?

I will be eternally grateful to God for giving us Fr. Aloysius.

[4] Shortly after her marriage, the young Stella Sanchez, whom I have known for forty years, was diagnosed by a specialist as sterile. She and her husband Robert resigned themselves to never having children. They went to Father Aloysius's Mass, and announced to him they had been married for six months. Father looked at them kindly and asked if they were expecting a child. "No," they replied, but did not reveal the reason (i.e., sterility). Father then blessed Stella, telling her with great conviction, "You will have a child in nine months!" A month later, and only from curiosity, Stella took a pregnancy test, and it came out positive! She and her husband then returned to Father. Upon sighting them at a distance, he exclaimed, "I know! You are already pregnant." A little girl was born to them exactly nine months after the blessing. Since then, Stella has had three more children.

[5] I drove Father to a hospital about a half hour east of Los Angeles to visit Mrs. Winifred Zimmerman who was seriously sick with lung problems and on the point of being transferred to another hospital. The woman could hardly breathe. A transparent oxygen tent was drawn over her body. Father spoke with her as I gazed over his shoulder. He repeatedly blessed her and told her with complete assurance that she would be perfectly fine and to definitely not worry anymore. Exhausted, but filled with joy, she nodded her head. She was transferred to another hospital within a few hours.

Approximately a week later she laughingly told us that upon arriving at the second hospital the medical personnel took new x-rays and compared them with those coming from the former hospital. They were visibly upset and began calling the first hospital to complain that they had sent someone else's x-rays. The woman several times tried to interject, "There is no mistake about the x-rays—it was God who healed me!" But just as many times they told her emphatically to be quiet, so that they could continue arguing with the first doctors. "Those angry doctors!" she chuckled. "They simply would not listen to me."

[6] My uncle, Walter Carpenter, whose heart was damaged in childhood from rheumatic fever, was admitted when he was about fifty-five years old to Veterans Hospital (Sawtelle) in West Los Angeles with a heart attack. The doctors could do nothing more for him and death seemed to be approaching quickly. Father Aloysius was called to the hospital. Father started multiplying blessings over my uncle's chest while my uncle was either comatose or deeply asleep. Afterward, my uncle related to us that suddenly he perceived a light streaming down toward him as if through a long tunnel, and at the top, in the light, he could see Father's face becoming clearer and clearer. He said Father's voice called him out of what seemed to be the deepest and darkest pit, while strength came pouring into his body from above. Restored at that moment to complete health, he was released from the hospital. He lived for many more years.

[7] The following case was related to me by Mrs. Michael Jones from Orange County who attended the Guild Masses. She said her husband, for lack of faith, never accompanied her to Mass. Michael had been seriously injured in a helicopter accident in the Korean War. He could not walk because his vertebrae had been damaged, making it necessary for him to use a wheelchair. The doctors had operated on him three times and had always closed him up as impossible to repair. Finally, his wife's insistence convinced Michael to come, "just once," to the Guild Mass, and give God a chance. Father passed by Michael among

those who lined up for a blessing. Father asked him if he had faith in Jesus Christ. When the disabled man answered "Yes," Father thundered the exact same injunction of the Apostles: "In the Holy Name of Jesus Christ, stand up and walk!" To the amazement of everyone present, the man immediately stood up and started walking around. It was a great privilege for me to see him in perfect health at subsequent Guild Masses.

[8] During the few months I answered the front door in the evenings, I remember several times leading a young couple, by the last name of Cernek, across the lounge to the chapel. Their faces were filled with sadness. The wife had terminal cancer and was showing no signs of improvement. Since they were returning for blessings every ten or fifteen days, I soon realized she was not getting any better, so my sorrow for them steadily increased. My only recourse was to tell them each time they left, "You never know. Sometimes God may wait a long time to answer prayers. Please, do come back." But inside me, I felt unsure whether I was preparing even greater disappointments for them. In my dilemma, I confided to Father Aloysius what I had been doing to foster their hopes each time they left.

Finally, on what seemed their eighth or ninth visit, this time, after receiving the blessing again, they returned to the front door radiant with joy, accompanied by Father Aloysius. When they left, Father confided to me with a sense of joyful relief, "At last, God healed the woman completely! I had begun to feel ridiculous in encouraging them to come back!"

[9] Ron Eason of Napa, California, was diagnosed in 1970 with Hodgkin's Disease: cancer of the lymphatic system. He was twenty-three years of age. At my request he wrote, on

July 16, 2000, a full account of his cure. It is worth reading in its entirety because it shows the personal attention Father bestowed on the sick. At the same time, it shows how difficult it is for a doctor to declare "miracle."

I first heard of Father Aloysius in the spring of 1970. I was having a discussion with Jeannine Susann Coelho (my future wife) and her family when the subject of miracles came up. I said that I'd never personally heard of any miracles, and they all said that they had a story I needed to hear. They proceeded to tell me about the cure of Christopher Bacich (my wife's nephew) who was born with cancer of the liver. He had been cured by God through Father Aloysius in 1969.

During mid-1970, I found that I had very little energy. I felt unusually tired nearly all the time and I would perspire heavily without exertion. I was an aviation electronics technician in the U.S. Navy, stationed at Moffett Field in Mountain View, California. Jeannine lived with her family in Pleasant Hill, California. In September, I had asked Jeannine to marry me and our nuptial Mass was scheduled for November 28th, the day before her twentieth birthday. One day that fall, she touched the right side of my neck while I was driving and I felt a sharp pain and a deep aching sensation. We decided that I needed to see a Navy doctor to find out about the pain.

The doctor examined me and scheduled the biopsy of the lymph node at the base of my neck, on the right side. On Thursday, November 26th, Jeannine accompanied me to a follow-up appointment with the doctor. He told us that the biopsied lymph node was malignant and that I'd been diagnosed with Hodgkin's disease: cancer of the lymphatic system. He said that some people have lived for twenty years with this form of cancer.

Jeannine later told me that she had never considered canceling our wedding but she did know something about cancer. Her thought was: "Well, I'll have a good husband for six months and then I'll be a widow at twenty!" She was prepared to make this huge sacrifice.

We were married as planned and I was admitted to Oak Knoll US Naval Hospital in Oakland, California, two days later, on Monday, November 30th. Tests were done and I was scheduled for exploratory surgery the following week. They planned to see how far the cancer had spread and to remove my spleen and a piece of my liver.

My wife had encouraged me to pray to St. Jude Thaddeus, the Saint of impossible cases. Then she said she was going to take me to see Father Aloysius. I was able to check out of the hospital for the weekend and we flew to Los Angeles on Friday evening, December 4th. We stayed with Jeannine's brother, George Coelho, who lived in Huntington Beach with his wife Barbara and their three children.

On Saturday, December 5th, we attended Father's Mass at the Claretian Monastery at 1119 Westchester Place in Los Angeles. I approached Father Aloysius as he was blessing the crowd and Jeannine and I explained my situation. Father blessed us and asked us to return on Sunday morning so that he could offer the holy sacrifice of the Mass for us.

That Saturday afternoon we went to the beach. I had an unexplained burst of energy and ran all over the beach without being exhausted. I had been without that kind of stamina for several months. We stayed there until evening.

On Sunday, December 6th, we returned to the monastery for Mass with Father Aloysius. However, he told us that he had been denied permission to celebrate a private Mass. He suggested we attend Mass at a nearby parish and then return to see him.

After Mass we went back to the monastery and Father took Jeannine and me to the chapel. Only the three of us were there with Jesus in the tabernacle. The chapel was constructed in-the-round with large glass windows on its exterior walls. There was a glass skylight in the center of the open-beam ceiling, directly above the altar. A large crucifix was suspended underneath the skylight, with the tabernacle and altar below. The day was dark and gloomy with no trace of sunlight.

As Father blessed me and prayed over me, he handed me several relics to venerate: a piece of the true cross, a relic of St. Peter, a relic of St. Anthony Mary Claret (the founder of the Claretian Order) and relics of a few other saints. When he blessed me, he embraced me as I knelt in front of him. I had the very clear sensation that all the rest of the world disappeared when Father embraced me and it seemed as though the two of us were suspended somewhere between heaven and earth. I experienced that same sensation every time I had the privilege to be blessed by Father Aloysius.

After the blessing, Father went up to the altar. He knelt in front of the tabernacle and placed his hand on its door. He prayed out loud, "Oh Jesus, please cure Ronald James Eason..." At that moment, *an intense light streamed into the chapel from the skylight!* The whole chapel was illuminated. Jeannine and I looked at each other in amazement as, in that same instant, we noticed that the weather outside the large windows was still dark and gloomy! The heavenly light lasted for a short time and then disappeared.

Father Aloysius finished his prayer and then told me to go ahead with the surgery if the doctors insisted but, he assured us, "They won't find anything." He asked me to promise to avoid mortal sin and to pray the Rosary every day. I promised. Then, Father reached into his pocket and gave me a beautiful wooden Rosary which had been given to him by Pope Paul VI.

No words can adequately describe the awesome peace that I felt when we returned to the Navy hospital with the prospect of surgery in the next few days. I was almost afraid to really believe that God had cured such an unworthy creature in that instant in Father's chapel. However, I was convinced that no cancer would be found.

On Monday, December 7th, more tests were done in preparation for the surgery. That afternoon the doctor entered my room, shaking his head. When I asked what was wrong, he said, "The blood test for mononucleosis is the simplest test there is. All last week your tests were negative. Today the test is positive and indicates that you're coming out of an acute case of mononucleosis. It doesn't make any sense. The tests should have been positive last week." I proceeded to tell him about our prayers and the blessing I received from Father Aloysius. He just said, "Well, I guess anything's possible!" and left the room. The surgery was canceled and I was discharged from the hospital.

For five years after my cure, I was susceptible to strep throat and any other throat illnesses that came along. After that, there were no related problems.

We later learned that many people my age had been diagnosed with various types of cancer, because in 1948 when I was born, the doctors were concerned about babies being born with enlarged thymus glands and I was one of them. My parents were instructed to take me for radiation treatments to reduce the thymus. The doctors later learned that the situation was not abnormal and the therapy was discontinued. The radiation was believed to be associated with the cancers that later developed.

My mother worked for a doctor in northern California. She informed me about the radiation–cancer connection and suggested I have a checkup. She never really believed that I had been cured. I told Father Aloysius of the situation and he wrote my mother a letter explaining that God had miraculously healed me.

[10] Ron Eason's wife, Jeannine, also benefited from a cure. Following is her husband's testimony of it as included in the document I received from him:

In April of 1970, Jeannine was working at a woman's retail clothing store and doing the display decorations: dressing mannequins and making the window and the interior trim look its best. Although she was only 5'1" tall and 115 pounds, part of her job was to lift and move the mannequins by herself. She had experienced severe back pain and consulted her doctor. An x-ray revealed a birth deformity: part of one of her vertebrae was missing. She was fitted with a stiff back brace and informed that she'd never be able to carry children because of the deformity and the resultant pain.

She visited Father Aloysius in Los Angeles that month and explained her situation to him. He took her into a room and blessed her back. The pain immediately disappeared and she never again wore the back brace.

Between 1971 and 1984, she had nine pregnancies.

[11] The following story was written by Neil Zarske of Huntington Beach, California. To verify the facts contained in it, I wrote to Louis Kaczmarek, the custodian of the International Pilgrim Virgin, and to the parents of the patient. All of them testified with letters to the truth of Mr. Zarske's statement. The sickness involved is called Kawasaki Disease (Mucocutaneous Lymph Node Syndrome).

In March, 1979, Louis Kaczmarek and the International Pilgrim Virgin Statue were in the Diocese of Orange, California. Lou knew that his brother's little boy, Matthew Louis, was very sick. On Friday, March 16, 1979, Lou got a phone call from his brother, from Michigan, saying that little Matthew Louis was so sick that he might die at any moment. Lou was afraid that he might get called back to Michigan for the funeral, and that he would not be able to finish his tour with the International Pilgrim Virgin Statue.

On March 20, Louis asked a local friend, Glenn, to invite Father Aloysius to come to see the statute, because Lou wanted to talk to Father. The following day...

When Lou and I returned to the church at 10:30 AM, this friend, Glenn, had brought Father Aloysius to see Lou. Father Aloysius said that if he could get to a phone, he would bless little Matthew Louis over the phone. Father Aloysius, Glenn, Lou, and I went back to the Zarske house to have Father Aloysius use the phone. Glenn made the telephone contact to the hospital back in Michigan. The closest Glenn was able to make the phone contact, was to the nurse on the same floor that Matthew Louis was on, whose name was Ann. Glenn asked for a Catholic nurse, to be able to relay the message, when he wasn't able to find Matthew Louis's parents at the hospital. Ann said she was a fallen-away Catholic. Glenn told her that Father Aloysius was going to bless little Matthew Louis over the phone, then handed the phone over to Father Aloysius. Father spent about five minutes on the phone, saying various prayers, through the intercession of Our Lady and Saint Michael, and making the Sign of the Cross many times, as he stood in the direction of and pointing toward Michigan. Ann felt Father's graces so much that she began crying on the phone. Glenn took the phone back from Father Aloysius, briefly talked to Ann, then hung up. Later that day, we found out that right after Father Aloysius's blessing, little Matthew Louis got up from his bed and went running down the hall of the hospital for the first time since his paralysis. Two days later Matthew Louis went home completely cured, of what had been diagnosed as a "No Cure, Paralyzing, and Death–Causing" disease.

A letter from Mrs. Susan Kaczmarczyk, the mother of Matthew Louis, was also received to confirm the above report. Her letter is included in the Appendices.

[12] Mrs. Beatrice McAteer of Boulder City, Nevada, narrated to me the following cure of her sixteen-year-old daughter, Dorothy. In 1959 the family lived in Inglewood, California. Dorothy had cancer of the throat and lymph nodes, which had started in June or July of that year. Here is Beatrice's story:

> I took Dorothy to the doctor (Irvin Kaye, MD), who told me it was cancer. So, I took her to a cancer specialist, who diagnosed her as having Mesenchymoma. All this time I did not tell Dorothy what she had so as not to grieve her even more. After being operated on to remove a tumor from her throat, it was necessary to give her radiation treatments, which appeared to have no good effect. The cancer specialist told me my daughter did not have a 50-50 chance, but no chance at all, and that she would not live six months. I continued to take her to radiation treatments, four or five times. She was throwing up from these treatments, and blood was coming out. She looked like death.
> I used to say three rosaries every night, praying for her cure. A neighbor told me about Father Aloysius. We went

over there, for the first time, on a Sunday. I had never seen Father Aloysius nor known of him before. There were at least one hundred people there, and Fr. Aloysius walked right over to my daughter, and he knew her throat was bad (even though nothing showed on the outside). He blessed her throat.

After a few more Sunday visits to Fr. Aloysius, I told him all about my daughter's illness and the radiation treatments she was receiving. He told me to quit the treatments; that she was going to be all right. I quit the treatments, because they were so painful for my daughter and I figured she was going to die anyway. The following Wednesday (after Father had told me to stop my daughter's treatments) I had a vision in my sleep. I saw the Blessed Mother who was smiling at me and dressed all in white. I woke up immediately, but she had disappeared. The following weekend I went to see Father again, and he told me Dorothy was cured.

When I went back to the doctor, he couldn't believe his eyes. My daughter was found to have no cancer at all, and Father Aloysius said she'll never have cancer again.[14]

[13] The following cure was received by Father Aloysius himself about eight years before I met him. I include it because it shows the importance of fervent and unrelenting prayer in obtaining favors from God. Father used to tell people about this case to encourage belief in the personal presence of the Blessed Mother in our lives.

On many occasions Father had required hospitalization, especially during the last twenty years of his life. On

---

[14] Beatrice's daughter, Dorothy Topf, tells me she was not informed at the time of the gravity of her case, because her mother did not wish to cause her more suffering than she was going through. Dorothy says her mother, who is now eighty-five years of age, has perfect lucidity and an excellent memory. Dorothy's cousin, Roger Delangis, who is a friend of mine, also testified to the truth of these events.

August 5, 1961, he entered St. John's Hospital in Santa Monica and was scheduled for major surgery on August 11th. He was going to be operated on inside the back portion of his skull in order to remove a tumor. The surgeon, Dr. Robert McKenna, told him the chances were enormous of his coming out of the operation as a vegetable, but that the operation was definitely needed. So Father decided to pray from that moment "right to the end." Complete x-rays had been taken more than once. Late in the night before the operation, he started reciting what he hoped would not be the last rosary in his life. When he arrived at the second Joyful Mystery, he pleaded with all his might to the Blessed Mother: "My dearest Mother! Cure me of this brain tumor. If you do so, I will dedicate the rest of my life teaching all souls how you are spiritually present to each human being in the most intimate way." Unceasingly he begged her. Then suddenly a warmth was experienced in his skull, at the very spot of the cancer. The Blessed Mother, he told us, was actually touching him on that spot. The next morning, he called for the nurse and said he wanted x-rays done over again. Because the operation was to take place within minutes, this was an upsetting favor to ask. "Please! Take just one more x-ray!" he implored with all his heart. So, x-rays were repeated and shortly afterwards the doctor came in and knelt down at Father's bedside with tears in his eyes, saying, "Father! The tumor has completely disappeared! It's a miracle! It's a miracle! I find no other explanation for this!"[15] The doctor then asked for Father's blessing.

---

[15] This narration is based on what I heard from Father Aloysius *himself*, except for the exact dates, for which I am most grateful to Mr. Jeffrey Moynihan (*Wonder Worker in America*, pp. 29-30).

AFTER RELATING THESE amazing incidents of God's mercy, I would like to point out three characteristics in healing ministry that regularly accompanied Father's pastoral concern for the sick and the dying.

First, Father recognized the risks involved for the faithful in healing the sick. One danger was the indiscreet zeal of those who attributed such cures to Father himself. He often needed to utter disclaimers. Sometimes after Mass (before the blessings took place) he would beg those present, "If anyone tries to attribute such a thing to me, please know that I have *nothing* to do with it! It is *God alone* who restores any sick person to health."

Second, does healing imply that God changes His mind? Is it childish superstition to "bargain" with God? At the beginning of a personal blessing, Father very often asked the afflicted person to promise something to God in order to give God some strong reason for reversing the laws of nature. He did not suggest anything material but, depending on the person's faith, something over and above their accustomed spiritual practices. For example, on several occasions Father asked persons who had lived away from the sacraments, "If God heals you, do you promise to do your level best to stay in the state of grace?" What formerly had seemed to them such a heavy burden now appeared incredibly light. For this reason, I saw numerous fallen-away Catholics fully restored to physical health. Many fervent souls, on the other hand, walked away accepting their crosses as the Will of God. While the latter made me realize the value of suffering, the former taught me that we might change God's Will by first changing ourselves.[16] I also was aware of a few who did not stick to their promises. One man, after having been cured twice, returned twice to his former life of sin. He pleaded to be healed a third time. Father could not bring himself to beseech God for another cure. Rather, he admonished the sick man, but with great gentleness, knowing well that the tendency to abuse God's patience is so much a part of human nature.

Third, in the ministry of healing, although some bargaining may take place, often the bill is handed to the priest. The priest's vocation is an imitation of Christ who was victim for our sins. The priest participates in the passion of Christ and publicly proclaims this oneness at the Consecration in the Mass: "This is My Body, which will be given up for you." What each day he proclaims at the altar, inevitably he will live out in his own flesh, if he is true to his priesthood. Father Aloysius's life was saturated with suffering, which he willingly accepted so that all souls, particularly those who asked for his prayers, might be favored by the Divine Physician. Some of the suffering came through grave misunderstandings. Doctors whose medical analyses had been contradicted occasionally became infuriated. This possibility is clear in the case of Mrs. Zimmerman, and can be subtly detected in the case of Maria Cucalon. In the latter case, Father, not unfamiliar with doctors' vexation and mindful about contradicting medical authorities, tells the woman: "If you wish to have the operation, please go ahead, but you don't need it." The same is evident in the case of Ron Eason (where the doctor's

---

[16] In Pope John Paul II's *Salvifici Doloris*, those faithful persons who suffer in any way are placed at the vanguard of the Church.

diagnosis changed to mononucleosis, even though, for the doctor himself, this was scientifically incomprehensible). Another kind of suffering is more obvious: physically taking on the sicknesses of others. When Father laid his hands upon their heads, many persons reported a flow of warmth or a strong wind that rushed downward from the peak of their skull through to the soles of their feet. Might we ask ourselves if he himself felt some concomitant flow—and perhaps painful—in the opposite direction that intimated to him what was taking place in the one he blessed?[17]

(III) **The gift of levitation.** Levitation was not something I personally witnessed in Father Aloysius. In fact, during his lifetime, whenever anyone would tell me about it, I was tempted to believe this was coming from their own imagination. When people are predisposed emotionally to see or hear something out of the ordinary, they may perceive it. The power of suggestion is flagrant.[18]

---

[17] Father was ever vulnerable to sicknesses and had a lengthy list of medical interventions. On our pilgrimage, he refrained from going into the baths at Lourdes, although everyone else did. He said the last time he attempted to do so he came out sicker than he had gone in. Matthew's Gospel quotes the prophet Isaiah: *He himself bore our sicknesses away and carried our diseases* (Mt. 8:17b; cf. Is. 53:4). The footnote of the New Jerusalem Bible explains: "Matthew takes the phrase to mean that Jesus 'took away' these sorrows by his healing miracles. This interpretation, at first sight forced, is in fact profoundly theological."

[18] This untoward attitude is aptly described by Ronald Knox as "ultrasupernaturalism." "The enthusiast," he explains, "expects more evident results from the grace of God than we others"... "He decries the use of human reason as a guide to any sort of religious truth. A direct indication of the Divine will is communicated to him at every turn." See:

After Father's death, some of the cases that were retold have sometimes more, sometimes less, credibility.[19] However, I would like to include a reported levitation that seems to me to carry sufficient reliability.

Mrs. Frances Collins of Phoenix, Arizona, has been a good friend of mine for approximately thirty-five years. Shortly after Father Aloysius's death, I began visiting her and her family when passing through Phoenix on my way to and from Los Angeles. For over ten years she never mentioned anything about Father's levitating. Not only is she not the kind of person to volunteer such information, she is even less given to discuss extraordinary phenomena. She appears to have a healthy dose of skepticism in her approach to life and, even more important, prefers listening to talking. On one occasion, when we were talking about Father Aloysius, whom she and her family had known well during his assignment in Phoenix (1963–1966), she touched upon the subject almost by accident. I did not understand what she meant by her astounding "surprise" in Fatima where I had first met her in August, 1972. "You were present!" she exclaimed. "You must know what I am referring to."

Ronald Knox's *Enthusiasm* (Christian Classics: Westminster, MD, 1983 [reprint of 1951 edition]), pp. 2–3.

[19] Concerning reported levitations and bilocations in Father Aloysius's life, see Patricia Treece's *The Sanctified Body* (Liguori, MO: Triumph Books, 1993), pp. 78-79, 218-219, 239, 245, 248-251, 257 (footnotes), 261-262, 265 (notes), 270, 373-375. I knew most of the witnesses interviewed by Treece and I believe her presentation is trustworthy and un-exaggerated.

I could not remember anything special and I asked her to please explain. Fighting embarrassment, she recounted what she had seen. When she had finished, I asked Frances if possibly there was some optical illusion involved; maybe the cassock itself had made Father appear not to touch the ground. "Absolutely not," she replied, repressing an urge to laugh. "It was too obvious to be an optical illusion." Even to this day, evidently she finds it humorous for anyone to be walking off the ground. She does not talk about the case unless urged to do so. Twenty years ago I asked her to compose a written statement, which follows:

> We were on a guided tour and the guide gave us only two hours to visit Fatima. A Mass was being said in the Chapel of the Apparitions. It was very crowded and we could not see the celebrant. Later we were happy to see that it was Father Ellacuria when we received Holy Communion from him. After Mass, Father Ellacuria and his aide were heading towards their quarters. As they were walking I, Frances, noticed that Father was about three or four inches off the ground. I wanted to speak to him, but at the same time did not want to interrupt him. But our time was so limited I feared we would not have a chance to speak to him. When I called to him, he turned and then he was back on the ground. We spoke to him briefly and then he departed with his aide, heading for the basilica.
>
> It was a wonderful and moving experience to see Father. One I shall never forget.[20]

(IV) **Significant coincidences.** When Father was not busy with work, for example, when traveling in a car, he would pray. If we were not saying the rosary together, his lips

---

[20] From Mrs. Frances Collins' signed document, December 8, 1999, in the files of our Order.

nevertheless were in quiet motion and his eyes remained shut as he appeared engaged in spiritual communication. "All heaven is around us," he often explained in his sermons. "And all the angels and saints are so close to each of us." He, who had been blessed in his childhood with hearing the rustling of angels' wings at night, hardly could have thought otherwise.[21]

With so firm a conviction in him, it should surprise no one that Father desired an effective relationship with the heavenly court at all times, to receive from the Church Triumphant all the help he could get. Such assistance was so varied that it is difficult to classify, and thus I lump it together as "the miracles in which God prefers to remain anonymous." Such heavenly works of art are related by Jeff Moynihan in various places in his exciting book, *Father Aloysius, Wonder Worker in America.* When I first pointed out some of Jeff's cases to our seminarians, I had to clarify to them that these took place in the eleven months during which Jeff accompanied Father Aloysius. None of it surprised me, because during the almost four years I lived under the same roof with Father, such things became more and more obvious. I learned to keep my eyes open, not for miracles in the strict sense, but rather for what Chesterton would have called the extraordinary in the ordinary.[22]

---

[21] This I learned from Father himself. Jeff Moynihan also mentions it in his book: "I asked Father if he ever noticed anything super natural as a child. He said 'yes'. At times he heard the miraculous sound of wings hovering above his head at night, when he was in bed. For him, this sound was a sign of the presence of his guardian angel" (*Wonder Worker in America,* p. 8).

[22] "Ordinary things [. . .] are more extraordinary" (*Orthodoxy* [Garden City, NY: Doubleday Image Books, 1959], 46).

[1] It was the evening of July 22, 1970 (one year after Father had returned to Los Angeles from his six-year "exile" to San Antonio and Phoenix).[23] We were heading for a special Mass which was to be presided over by the Cardinal with numerous other priests, concelebrating. Late getting onto the Harbor Freeway, we soon found ourselves bottled up in a traffic jam that seemed interminable. How would we ever get to the Cathedral? "If we pray to St. Michael the Archangel," Father said, "he certainly will get us there on time." We said prayers to the angelic opponent of Lucifer, and Father raised his hand and blessed the highway in front of us. The traffic jam immediately started loosening up and we were soon free to zoom into downtown. I left Father at the sacristy and walked into the front door of the Cathedral, only to see Father, complete with alb and stole, stepping out from the sacristy and making the genuflection in front of the main altar—in complete unison with the other priests who had filed in from the front door!

As we drove home, Father delighted in telling me how, when that ceremony concluded, one of the more important Chancery monsignors, not having seen Father since before his "exile" to Phoenix and San Antonio, had approached and, scrutinizing Father Aloysius from head to foot, had gasped, "You have resurrected! You have resurrected!"

[2] During our two-year sojourn in Fatima (1971–73), Father and I arrived one night together in August of 1972 from Portugal, at Kennedy International Airport in New

---

[23] The period spent in Texas and Arizona between 1963 and 1969 was considered by many people, including Father himself, as an exile. We will treat this period later on.

York. The fifteen or more immigration lines were exceedingly long. We took our place at the very end of one of these lines. Shortly afterward, I noticed something I could hardly believe. The guard at the front of the line was beckoning to us with his hands. In such official circumstances, I could make no sense of what he wished to convey. Then everyone else began beckoning together with the guard—they wanted us to come forward. We had no choice but to creep forward—something like remorseful spaniels—right up to the front of the line! People who live back East say this is not so unusual in New York. But even allowing for this deference of Irish cops, I was amazed that it was not just the cop, but the whole queue.

[3] In Fatima, Portugal, we as seminarians usually surrounded Father wherever he went. One day around noon, we stepped out of our VW bus and were approaching a house (the Casa of the Holm Oak) that was flanked by a rock garden. Somehow Father fell, with all his weight, backwards into the rocks. The fall produced a resounding impact that frightened us because of Father's already very delicate health. We lifted him up, worriedly soliciting him about his well-being. He calmly replied that everything was fine, not even the slightest pain. It was as if *nothing* had happened. During several days, in our bewilderment we would often ask each other, "Did you hear that tremendous crash when Father fell?" As fervent novices we unanimously agreed that the devil was out to kill him, but his angels were bodyguards cushioning the hardest fall.

[4] Whenever Father happened to find himself suddenly out of place, for example, if accidentally and uninvited he walked into a domain where he, in his humility, perceived himself a nuisance, he became fearful about disturbing

whatever else was going on. (I recall during the years I lived in Spain, that people considered any "attention drawing" to be a real no-no in social etiquette.) His solution was to ask his guardian angel to make him invisible. Successfully weathering these situations—an essential for someone as well-known as he was—depended on passing by everyone unnoticed. Now, the lounge of the Claretian Provincial House, situated as it was—right in the center of all adjoining rooms—was an ideal place for prominent gatherings. As such, it often became a testing ground for anyone's etiquette, usually involving trying to extricate oneself from a lengthy conversation that was intended to be only a passing greeting. For these and numerous other cases, Father suggested the easiest way, which he claimed always worked: "Just ask the Guardian Angels to make you invisible and march on!" Thanks to this tactic, which had become automatic to him, Father had more time to visit the sick in the afternoons.[24]

[5] A favorite job for Father's angel was to prepare the "dispositions" (i.e., the emotional attitude) of the "indisposed" people we sometimes deal with in life. If anyone had been ruffled, for example, by a serious disappointment, Father would pray to his guardian angel to approach the guardian angel of that same person, and ask him to replace vexed feelings in his subject with benign and favorable sentiments. Hoping everything would come off all

---

[24] Recently one of my ex-seminarians passed over to the United States. Afterwards he related to me that he had an extremely dangerous passing. He remembered our Father Founder's injunction, then prayed to his guardian angel for a miracle, and walked slowly past the control tower "invisible".

right in such delicate encounters, he first would arm himself with fervent prayers to his guardian angel. Then he trudged the minefield in his approach to what—judging by surrounding "catastrophic" circumstances—normally might have produced very hostile reactions. Upon finding the angels had obtained the desired effect, Father would come away, exultantly grateful about how propitious the circumstances or the person had turned out. Father recommended we use our guardian angels for these and equally perplexing challenges, big or small, in life.[25] From experience, he learned that guardian angels want nothing more than to be put to work.

[6] After a few months of driving for Father Aloysius, one afternoon, just after we rolled up the ramp onto the 405 Freeway in Sherman Oaks, a traffic cop pulled me over. He asked me to get out of the car and stand at the front left fender. He explained to me how I had passed another car under the freeway overpass before turning right onto the freeway on-ramp. He told me he had no other alternative than to write up a ticket. He asked for my driver's license. I walked back to the front door of the car to get my license

---

[25] In theological treatises on the Angels we can verify this angelic function. The Angels can influence our emotional life, for example by instilling uplifting images into persons who suffer from anxiety or sadness. "Illumination of man's mind is the most direct and most constant effect of the angelic tutelage; according to St. Thomas (S. Th., I, Q. cxiii, art. 5, ad 2), it is not too much to say that the human race is kept in mental equilibrium through the unceasing watchfulness of the good spirits" (Anscar Vonier, O.S.B., "The Angels" in: *The Teaching of the Catholic Church*, Vol. I [New York: the Macmillan Company, 1955], p. 271).

out of the glove compartment. Father Aloysius asked what was the problem. I answered: "He is giving me a ticket." Father answered, "I will say three Hail Mary's so that he does not!" When I heard that, I thought, *No way. It's useless and too late because this cop has already opened up his little pad of tickets, and he's determined to do what he has a mind to do.* I handed my driver's license to the officer. He looked hard and long at the photograph taken several months before I had met Father Aloysius. Then he looked up at me, and said, "Is this *you*?" Yes, I replied. He shook his head in disbelief and said essentially, but in his own words, what Our Lord said to the adulterous woman in John 8: "Go, and sin no more!" (I will leave it to your imagination what I looked like in my "Old Testament" days, a university student from the mid-60s.)

III.

Origins

The difficulty I had in uncovering anything about Father Aloysius's childhood can readily be appreciated if we consider Father's attitude toward his past. He never volunteered information about his youth and I interpreted this as from fear of disloyalty about "looking back" (Lk. 9:62), a dread undoubtedly inculcated during his formative years in religious life. On May 28, 1976, he gave me a five-page résumé of his past life—a photocopy of a form which his own superiors had handed to him and other members of his congregation to fill out for the official files. This is all I possess concerning his religious and priestly "curriculum vitae." It resembles an obsolete application form for a job and carries the bare essentials. Any other information I have, comes from a letter from one of his classmates, which I quote later on, as well as what amounts to loot resulting from some questions I ventured to ask out of curiosity and which Father answered with utmost brevity. These answers, since they are brief and obliging, led me to conclude that to delve further would have been an indiscretion on my part. So, unable to descend to greater details, I must resign myself to delivering only a sketch of those early years.

Father Aloysius Ellacuria was born on June 21, 1905, in the small village of Yurre, approximately 26 kilometers southeast of Bilbao, in the heart of the Basque country of

Spain. He was the fourth of nine children born to Ramón Ellacuria (1873–1920) and Marta Echevarria (1874–1950). He was baptized on the very next day as Juan Luis (Luis = Aloysius, in honor of being born on the feast of St. Aloysius Gonzaga).

That year, June 22 happened to be the solemn feast of Corpus Christi, the greatest Eucharistic feast in the liturgy. The town church was splendidly decorated and many people were still lingering after Mass when Father's parents approached the baptismal font. Someone in the baptismal party (his own grandmother, if I remember correctly), quite impressed by these unusually sacred circumstances, exclaimed: "For heaven sake! This little boy must be called to the priesthood!"

Ramon Ellacuria's occupation was, in Father's own words, "a proprietor of farms, mountains and pastures and woody groves in and around Yurre."[1] When I journeyed to the little town of Yurre in 1978, I was struck by the picturesque surroundings which Father's words so graphically describe. Ramon was a third order Franciscan, and as such was buried in the habit of the Franciscans. Father said that many years after his father's death, the body was exhumed and found to be completely incorrupt.

Naturally the happiest day of Father Aloysius's childhood was his First Holy Communion, received on February 2, 1912. He was only six-and-a-half years old and

---

[1] From the five-page résumé referred to above (and hereafter) as "curriculum vitae."

was confirmed the following year. He tells us that during his childhood, the awakening of his vocation came when he observed from the window of his house the Franciscan friars in their brown habits, who sometimes would beg from door-to-door. The very sight of them in the religious habit instilled in him an ardent attraction to the religious life.

During his childhood, Father tended to be emotionally reserved. Evidently he spent most of his time indoors, because he was very attached to his mother, Marta, who conducted herself as a most tender mother and dutiful housewife for her large household. After her death, Father always considered her a saint, and used to tell us he had never asked anything through her intercession that was not granted.

When I visited the two-story house in Yurre where Father's ancestors had lived, I found Father's nephew Francisco, who was then forty years old, living there with his wife and children. I asked Francisco how old the house was and he, without stopping to tally, replied, "A thousand years." The house is made out of enormous stones and stands on a gentle slope. Downstairs there was a stone hearth upon which the family still cooked with wooden logs. They assured me it was their intention to acquire a gas stove as soon as possible. Upstairs I saw the large bed upon which Father was born. In Basque fashion, the house is separated from other homes in the area by rolling green meadows and lush, aromatic pine trees.

At eleven years of age, on Sunday, July 30, 1916, Father entered the Congregation of Missionary Sons of the

Immaculate Heart of Mary (Claretians). Previously he had felt an attraction to enter the Carmelites because of his awareness of a renowned nun, Thérèse of Lisieux, who, not long before, had died in the odor of sanctity. He admired her so much that he would have chosen her name in religious life if there had existed a Spanish equivalent in masculine gender (Latin: *Teresio*). It may surprise us in America that he should have entered the seminary so early. But even forty-five years ago (1973), when I studied at the Major Seminary of Burgos, Spain, there were at least 100 eleven-year-olds beginning at the Minor Seminary in Burgos each year. Why did he choose the Claretians and not the Franciscans or the Carmelites? He told me the Claretians one day showed up in Yurre and rounded up any boys who wanted to come along. (This practice was common in Catholic countries up to about sixty years ago.)

During Father's year as postulant (1919 to 1920), he constantly prayed to St. Rita of Cascia, "Saint of the Impossible," to obtain a miracle. What miracle? That he would actually make it through the year of trial and be accepted into the novitiate. In his humility, Father was convinced he was not fit for religious life and would never be approved by his Superiors. When, at the end of the year, it was announced that he actually had been accepted, he was stunned with disbelief. He told me this was sufficient proof that St. Rita well deserves her epithet "patroness of impossible cases." Father's attitude bewildered me. I could not imagine anything in him that would have disqualified him for religious life. But whenever he mentioned his postulancy, he would burst into intense thanksgiving to St. Rita for getting him through the year of probation. I remember his doing this again when we went on pilgrimage in October, 1970. Among the places visited was the shrine in Cascia with the incorrupt body of St. Rita. With profound sentiments of indebtedness, he knelt at her tomb and vehemently poured out his acknowledgments in front of everyone present.

In a letter dated January 6, 1992, a classmate of Father Aloysius, by the name of Father Miguel Atucha, CMF, who accompanied Father during the full thirteen years of his formation, recalls his early years in the seminary with Father Aloysius:

> During those four years [of minor seminary which concluded with the postulancy] I always saw Juan Luis dedicated to a life that was normal in every respect. What stood out in him were his simplicity, his piety, his kindness, and his dedication to study. I believe he knew how to fulfill quite well the role of a hidden and fragrant violet. Regarding his studies, he was outstanding for the special aptitude he had for languages and for writing.[2]

Upon completing the postulancy, on August 14, 1920, Father was clothed with the holy habit of the Claretians at the ceremony to commence the Novitiate. The

---

[2] Letter from Fr. Miguel Atucha, CMF, addressed to Fr. Javier Oroz, CMF, Tolosa, Jan. 6, 1992 [*translation mine*]. Quoted with permission of Fr. Oroz.

habit consists of a black, button-down cassock with sash. The habit always was very important to him, and he was almost never seen without it. He told us to wear our habit always, except on public transportation or during vigorous games.

About the Novitiate (1920–1921), Father Atucha writes:

> Since the building had to be adapted for the needs of a novitiate, it turned out to be a year of many discomforts on the material level. Of course, this did not adversely affect Juan Luis at all... If Juan Luis had dedicated himself to laying solid human and Christian foundations during the minor seminary or in the postulancy, he took great advantage of his novitiate year to empty himself completely into the perfect mold of his missionary vocation, which was both Cordimarian [i.e., Heart of Mary] and Claretian. I believe the novitiate year was for him a year both of extraordinary grace as well as unforgettable, a year that he undoubtedly carried within him for the rest of his religious life... How joyful and happy Juan Luis looked on that much awaited day of his first profession! How much he would have wished those vows, that oath, and that sacred consecration had been perpetual.[3]

Father reminded those who entered religious life later on that in the early part of the twentieth century the rules were very severe. Although he was in favor of rigorous renunciation, he was also of the opinion that some of it

---

[3] *Ibid*. Previous to the Code of Canon Law of 1917, perpetual vows were first and final.

could go too far. For example, when his own father died, Father Aloysius was still a postulant and only fourteen years of age. The fact that he was not allowed to attend his father's funeral appeared to him (at least in retrospect) to be heartless.

Besides the strictness of the rules, meals and accommodations were totally deficient. Cold, piercing winds from the Cantabrian Sea were typical, thus flues and throat maladies abounded. During one of his sicknesses, Father recalled his throat was stripped of all the inner lining, so he could not swallow saliva without flinching and remained awake every night from pain until the sickness abated. This memory may have inspired his love of Christ's thirst for souls from the Cross—*Sitio!*—the thirst he recommended us to cultivate toward all souls. The food in the seminary was totally inadequate. Even fifty years later, the Rector of the Seminary in Spain told me that if a seminarian were to eat only what is served regularly in the dining room, he would die of hunger. I was amazed that so small a country, much of which is covered with rocky soil, actually feeds fifty million people.

During the three years of philosophy (1921–1924), Father studied with his companions in Beire (Navarra). He told me they used to put on dramas inside the seminary. The purpose was to perfect the seminarians' eloquence in preaching and oratory. Those were his teenage years (16–19 years of age). He told me he was actually the best actor in the class during philosophical training. The dramatic trait remained in him all his life and provided a gripping quality to his homilies.[4] But as a teenager his acting ability could not mean he had become an extrovert, in any sense of the word. His school companion attests to the contrary:

> Juan Luis spent three years of philosophy, externally without hardly being noticed, as a hidden and fragrant violet. His tenacious work was interior, in his life of formation toward his full, future missionary and Cordimarian life. He was definitely convinced that no one can give what he does not have, and that the first and most difficult conquest is over oneself for God. We can summarize these three years of his life of religious formation in these words: Juan Luis, in the ordinary run of his daily life, appeared extraordinary by his constant faithfulness to all his duties.[5]

On June 22, 1926, the very anniversary of his baptism, Father professed perpetual vows. He was twenty-one years of age. He used to point out to us that for many of the Fathers of the Church, taking vows in religious life means a "second baptism"—sins committed before that day will not be considered at the Last Judgment.

Father's theological studies lasted six years and comprised: (1) three years of Dogmatic Theology in the

---

[4] In his homilies, Father often appeared to relive in himself the intense spiritual struggles gleaned from the Gospels and from the lives of the Saints. Using simple but bold facial and vocal skills, his pithy statements fell with power upon his hearers. Because his eyes were generally shut when preaching, if he opened them it only heightened the impact.

[5] Fr. Atucha.

Major Seminary of Santo Domingo de la Calzada (Logroño, Spain), for which he received his licentiate in 1927; (2) two years of Moral Theology in the Claretian Seminary of Segovia, Castile; (3) one year of Pastoral Theology in Aranda de Duero, which is one hour to the south of Burgos in the same province of Burgos. Father told us that these studies were equivalent to a doctoral degree in theology. All of the *Summa Theologica* had to be committed to memory.[6]

About the years of theology, Father's classmate recalls:

> ... Theological studies raised him higher and higher in divine and supernatural knowledge. He saw how one discovers right in front of him the infinite treasures that are endless, like divine constellations. He saw how all the riches

---

[6] St. Thomas Aquinas was strongly promoted at that time, especially from Pope Leo XIII's encyclical *Aeterni Patris* (1879) onward, until about 1960. Pope St. John Paul II, in his encyclical *Faith and Reason*, again promotes Thomistic philosophy. Nevertheless, in today's seminaries, we have become familiar with St. Thomas Aquinas only through significant quotations from his works. Maurice de Wulf (†1947), who wrote a *History of Medieval Philosophy*, said: "Scholasticism collapsed, not from a lack of ideas, but from a lack of brains!" After I became a priest I dedicated a few years to read the entire *Summa Theologica*. Such reading provides the experience to which Fr. Atucha refers: "He saw how one discovers right in front of him the infinite treasures that are endless." After St. Thomas's death (†1274), he was considered for sainthood, and the question was asked, "What miracle did he work?" The answer was immediate—"The *Summa Theologica*." In Catholicism, after the Bible, this is the best book in existence.

of these subjects were as nothing in view of faithfully fulfilling his mission as a Cordimarian and Claretian apostle in the footsteps of Jesus Christ and of St. Anthony Mary Claret. It was evident that Juan Luis did not feel immediately inspired to the external apostolate. Rather, he dedicated himself solely to interior prayer, sacrifices, and good example. He remembered well what St. Francis Xavier had once written to some Jesuit seminarians in Rome who were so eager about going as soon as possible to the missions in the Indies: "For now, your mission is right there, in Rome— and the mission is none other than your solid formation, so that later on you may be true apostles of Christ."[7]

Father was ordained in the chapel of the Faculty of Theology of Burgos on November 3, 1929, just prior to finishing his pastoral year.[8] He was twenty-four years of age. His first Holy Mass was celebrated on the following day in Aranda de Duero, fifty miles south of Burgos.

Father recalled that during the same year, while studying pastoral theology in Aranda de Duero, he was in close contact with three of the fifty-one future Claretian martyrs of Barbastro who were shot to death during the Spanish Civil War in August of 1936. The three were: his professor Father Juan Diaz Nosti; Father Sebastian Calvo Martinez who lived in the adjoining room; and John Pratts.[9]

---

[7] Fr. Atucha.

[8] He was ordained by the newly installed Archbishop of Burgos, Emmanuel De Castro. I am familiar with this chapel as I studied in the Faculty of Theology of Burgos for five years prior to ordination.

[9] I could not locate John Pratts among the fifty-one Claretian martyrs of Barbastro. Nevertheless, in the Spanish Civil War, more than 270 Claretian priests, brothers, and seminarians were executed. (See the

About eight months after ordination, Father was assigned to Panama. He arrived in Colon on October 9, 1930. In a letter to his confrères back in Spain, he finishes by saying: "We implore from our brothers of the Congregation some prayers so that God Our Lord and the Heart of His Holy Mother may straighten our path to the purest and the most perfect attainment of the threefold aim of our beloved Congregation by the threefold sacrifice which, because we are looking toward the heights, we have just made with the greatest joy: the sacrifice of our family, of our language, and of our country."[10]

Father remained at most six months in Panama, helping the "Rector of the Cathedral as his assistant, and as acting pastor on Sundays in Taboga Island, near Panama City." His assignment was soon changed to the United States. In his personal résumé, Father explains the reason for this change after such a short stay in Central America. He considered himself "far too immature to work immediately in the missions and unprepared to do pastoral work that early in life," written in what he called "my

---

very inspiring booklet *Claretian Martyrs of Barbastro* by Gabriel Campo Villegas, trans. Joseph Daries, CMF [Quezon City: Claretian Publications, 1998[2]]; and the breathtaking movie "Un Dios Prohibido," aired in 2013). During the Spanish Civil War of 1936–1939, and especially in the early months of the conflict, individual clergymen were executed while entire religious communities were persecuted, leading to a death toll of 13 bishops, 4,172 diocesan priests and seminarians, 2,364 monks and friars and 283 nuns, for a total of 6,832. (What most Americans know about the Spanish Civil War is limited to what Hemingway imagines about it in *For Whom the Bell Tolls*.)

[10] Letter from Colon, Panama (October 9, 1930).

personal humble exposition" to the General Government of the Claretian Congregation in Rome. He explained to his Superiors that he believed he was incapable of taking on such a difficult mission until "I [am] better prepared spiritually and pastorally." Simultaneous to Father's appeal, another letter arrived in Rome from the Rector of the Dominquez Seminary in Compton, California, expressing the urgent need "for a young priest very well versed in Latin, Spanish and mostly Greek" to teach the postulants.[11]

Father arrived at the Port of San Diego, California, on April 25, 1931. He began immediately teaching three different languages in Dominquez Seminary, particularly New Testament Greek. Many years ago, I asked Mrs. Alta Flocca, who knew Father Aloysius during that period of his life, what he was like as a young priest. She answered, "I used to drive all the way down from La Crescenta to Dominquez Seminary for spiritual direction each month. He would receive me in his office, and would never open his eyes when speaking to me. He was so recollected! He was so totally *apart* from this world, I couldn't believe it! It was well worth going out of my way, because in him I had really found a gem! In his younger years—contrary to the crowds we see around him nowadays—almost no one knew about him."

The Seminary environment provided the silence and solitude Father craved in order to develop a deeper interior

---

[11] All information signaled by quotation marks in this paragraph has been taken from Father's five-page curriculum vitae.

life. Anyone who has worked in the missions (or in any big city, for that matter) can fully appreciate Father's preference. The greatest danger for young priests is to believe that to "save souls at all cost" they must hurl themselves into feverish activity. The heresy of activism is nothing new but, unfortunately, today it seems to have become the norm.[12] Holiness cannot be improvised, but usually takes many years for development. As we have seen, this is something Father Miguel Atucha, during their earliest years of formation, holds up as one of Father Aloysius's essential characteristics.

Christ himself did not start his public life until after he had spent long years in Nazareth as an unknown carpenter. In most of the Saints, the active years were preceded by several years of meditation and purification of the heart in a "desert experience." St. Paul, for example, who received his call at twenty-four years of age, had to wait a further ten years in obscurity in Tarsus before he launched out—not on his own initiative, but invited by Barnabas—on what soon became a world mission.

Works like Dom Chautard's *The Soul of the Apostolate* and Louis Lallemant's *Spiritual Doctrine* were among Father's favorites. The former was highly recommended by

---

[12] In fact, Pope Benedict XVI stated that the heresy of our times is Pelagianism, the doctrinal aberration that places on man's shoulders all the responsibility for salvation (i.e., human nature considered as good enough without God's grace). This is why so little importance today is given to the Sacraments, particularly to Confession.

Pope St. Pius X.[13] Jean-Baptiste Chautard, OCSO (†1935), underlines the great necessity of a deep interior life as the only valid source from which the apostolate springs. To act otherwise not only is foolhardy but dangerous to oneself and to others. We are living through the consequences of this abandonment of prayer life: the great falling away of so many souls consecrated to God's work, and the consequent lack of new vocations.

St. Anthony Mary Claret, to express this paradoxical relation of action to contemplation, once wrote: "Today I have more work to do, therefore I must pray more." Father Aloysius, who took St. Anthony Mary Claret as his model, did his best to remain distanced from external activity until he had reached a union with Christ that would permit him to dedicate himself fully to apostolic work. That moment did not arrive until 1939–40. Prior to that year, he remained, metaphorically, in the humble abode of Nazareth. This period of preparation does not mean he passed time in idleness. As a young priest, Father was always very busy, principally with the formation of seminarians. But he spent as much time as he could in prayer. Such a lifestyle is possible for anyone, even when apostolic duties are pressing. It is a matter of knowing where to put the

---

[13] "I can offer you no better guide than the *Soul of the Apostolate*, by Dom Chautard, Cistercian Abbot. I warmly recommend this book to you, as I value it very highly, and have myself made it my bedside book" (words of Pope St. Pius X, in an audience granted in 1908 to Msgr. Cloutier, Bishop of Three Rivers, Canada).

emphasis in our lives.[14] Eventually, after a life spent in deep recollection, a person acquires the capacity to give himself fully to what is often called "apostolic irradiation." The final phase of the spiritual life is an undiminishing torrent of spiritual energy for the salvation of souls. The source of this energy is Christ Himself. This source becomes permanent for the apostolate when finally one can say in all sincerity, "It is no longer I who live, but Christ who lives in me" (Gal. 2:20). But even after that, one may still need to continue as something of a "sociable hermit."

The second work (i.e., Lallemant, †1635) became the basis of Father Aloysius's own spirituality. This classic is still placed among the ten greatest in Christian spirituality. It teaches that holiness operates between two poles: (1) by a thorough but ongoing purification of the soul, by which (2) one eventually becomes capable of distinguishing the delicate voice of the Holy Spirit within the conscience. Thus, mysticism is nothing other than complete and continual obedience to the breathing of the Holy Spirit. In practice, this is obtained through rectitude of intention. This interior experience of making choices with the right motive is also termed "purity of intention." Because the soul is now purified of other desires and fears (positive and negative

---

[14] St. Teresa in *The Way of Perfection* warns her Sisters about the temptation among beginners to give away all the fruit (of one's tree of holiness) to those whom one believes to be in greater spiritual need than themselves, instead of eating the first-fruits for personal growth.

appetites), God Himself guides the choices the soul makes, through infused (i.e., supernatural) prudence.

If I had to put Father's spirituality in a nutshell, I would call it "living totally refuged in the Immaculate Heart of Mary." Apart from the fact that I never knew of anyone more Marian than he, the attitude expressed by such a life of total abandonment to the Blessed Mother both demands and produces all of the above-expressed aspects of the spiritual life, which are summed up in the glorious freedom of the children of God.

IV.

Transformation

L ife in the minor seminary at the beautiful old
Dominguez hacienda was normal in every way
according to Father. There are only two events I recall him
mentioning to me connected with his teaching stint at
Rancho Dominguez: (1) The terrifying Long Beach
earthquake of March 10, 1933. While everyone evacuated
the buildings, he heard a seminarian scream at the top of his
lungs: "Confession! Confession!" (2) Once, at the beginning
of a fall semester, a new vocation, not familiar with the
words *seminary* and *cassock*, sent the following written
message to the rector: "I am coming to the cemetery, please
prepare a casket for me."

After two years in Rancho Dominguez, Father was
assigned to the Claretian seminary of Silver Peak in Walnut,
California, where again he was fully committed to the
formation of seminarians. He remained two years (1933–
35) and then was sent to St. Jude's Seminary in Momence,
Illinois (on the outskirts of Chicago).

Father remained in Momence from 1935–1942. He
later called these seven years his "golden years." Here is his
heavy work schedule: assisting the Prefect of Postulants;
teaching Greek and Latin and other subjects (for the first
two years); acting in the capacity of Superior and Prefect
(after 1937); fulfilling the duties of Vocational Director
(from 1939 on); teaching and confessing nuns at the

neighboring convents. About the large St. Jude's Seminary, Father states: "God helped me most providentially to save the life and vocations of the seminary."[1] Father had an outstanding talent for attracting vocations and helping young men, through his spiritual advice, to overcome all difficulties in their vocation. I believe Father's "apostolic irradiation" began during this period. In his curriculum vitae, Father states: "Those were my Golden Years to draw me very much closer to God."

In order for me to understand the full import of this last statement, I needed to do some spiritual reading, and then ask more questions.

In 1970, when I was living at the Claretian Provincial House, I discovered stacks of old spiritual books in the basement closet. I started reading great books like *The Conversions of the Soul* by R. Garrigou-Lagrange, OP, and other classics of traditional ascetic and mystical theology. These introduced me to the concept of "stages" in the spiritual life, particularly the way St. Teresa of Avila describes them in her Seven Mansions of the *Interior Castle*.

One day, overcoming my fear of invading Father's interior castle, I straightforwardly asked him if he had experienced such stages of the spiritual life. With complete calm he replied "yes." Seeing he was not ruffled by this question, I ventured to ask him if he had reached

---

[1] Curriculum vitae.

Transforming Union.[2] Appearing timid, but with full tranquility, he replied in the affirmative. "When did that come about?" I continued to pry.

---

[2] The Transforming Union corresponds to St. Teresa's Seventh Mansion of the Interior Castle. She herself received this grace at 57 (ten years before her death), after she had finished writing the *Life* and before writing the *Interior Castle* (written in 1577). In all, from the moment she firmly decided to become a saint (beginning with her overpowering experience upon beholding a statue of the scourged Christ in her convent), it took sixteen years to progress from the Fourth to the Seventh Mansion. This, in many respects, is a relatively short term to arrive at complete transformation.

The Transforming Union is a kind of deification of the soul. It is sometimes called "mystical marriage" because a soul from that moment on is irrevocably bonded to Christ, and is confirmed in grace. (The possibility of sinning is disputed by authors; even St. Teresa and St. John of the Cross are of differing opinion.) The soul, without losing its own identity, is divinized in such a way as to become a perfect instrument of Christ in this world. Both St. Teresa and St. John of the Cross speak at length of this grace, giving us to understand this as the culminating point of the spiritual journey (although certainly not the end). After this point, the soul launches out into active service without fear of impairing the interior life through excessive apostolic labor.

The life of prayer, then, is a progressively greater union with Christ, beginning with the union of wills in the Prayer of Quiet, corresponding to the Fourth Mansion. This prayer and the successive prayer stages are entirely gifts, to be received with great gratitude. We can do nothing to bring them about in us, but proper dispositions of the soul are a necessary condition. After the Fourth Mansion, if one is to persevere, one learns to welcome suffering with generosity. Because of its power to purify the soul, suffering speedily brings about conformity with Christ. This is the principal aim of the two Dark Nights (of the Senses and of the Spirit, respectively), which must be undergone with as much fortitude as possible.

"It was Holy Thursday, 1940, in a chapel in Manteno, Illinois." The chapel was part of Our Lady's Academy where the religious Sisters Servants of the Holy Heart of Mary taught. After Holy Mass, which he had just celebrated for the Sisters, Father knelt in front of the tabernacle to give thanks. He experienced a deep and inexpressible sensation of joy flooding his entire being. A devout young woman who was his penitent, and who would eventually take Perpetual Vows in the same order of nuns, was also attending the Mass with the others. Later she confided to Father that Our Lord had mystically shown her that something quite unusual had taken place. In a vision she had seen a light first depart from the tabernacle and then proceed to surround Father as a luminous silver cloud. He remained shrouded in this light for a short time when the cloud began to contract, finally reaching the size of his body, and then turning gold. The young woman's name was Frances Hennessey. She entered the convent on May 31, 1940, taking the name of Sister Mary Mediatrix.[3]

My questions continued. I learned that the experience just described above was preceded a year earlier (on Holy Thursday, 1939) by what St. Teresa calls "spiritual espousals," a stage of prayer corresponding to the Sixth Mansion of the Interior Castle, also called the

---

[3] Mr. Jeffrey J. Moynihan has written a book on her life, called *Sister Mary Mediatrix: A Mystic in America* (2012). Fr. Aloysius said: "Sister Mary Mediatrix was such a gift of God. Her influence changed my life completely."

Conforming Union. As a fully interior experience (i.e., without external manifestations), it is much more difficult to understand and even more difficult to express in words. Likewise, a year after the luminous experience of 1940, and also on Holy Thursday (April 10, 1941), Father received what perhaps is the highest mystical grace—the gift of retaining the Sacramental Species within one's breast. The same grace was received by St. Anthony Mary Claret, who miraculously retained the Sacred Species within his breast from one Holy Communion to another during the last nine years of his life.[4] During this third experience, immediately after the Consecration of the Holy Mass, Father felt a torrent of power flowing from the Sacred Species into his heart.

THE QUESTION ALWAYS COMES UP—How could anyone with such a gift be sure of its reality? In order not to deceive himself on a matter of such great importance, Father sometimes would ask God during his blessings upon sick persons to heal the individual, praying "... If you are truly present in my breast." He told me that whenever he added

---

[4] When the gift of continuous Sacramental Presence is received, normally it is to establish God's servant as a pillar against the unrestrained paganism of the times. This particular purpose is indicated by St. Anthony Claret in his notes for August 26, 1861, the day he received the sacramental species: "Por lo mismo...debo...hacer frente a todos los males de España" (*San Antonio Maria Claret: Escritos autobiograficos* [Madrid: B.A.C., 1981] p. 354, par. 694). This special gift was also received by St. Faustina Kowalska: "My heart is a living tabernacle in which the living Host is reserved" (*Diary*, 1302).

this motive to his own prayer *the person blessed was always cured.*

All three special graces—Conforming Union, Transforming Union, and the Sacramental Species—were experienced interiorly by Father Aloysius on the Holy Thursdays of 1939–1941. The day itself acquires great importance in Father's life for two further reasons: (1) The aim of his founding a new religious institute was to provide a place where the mysteries of Holy Thursday would be perpetuated; this was made clear to him on Holy Thursday of 1972, as we will relate in Chapter Six; (2) In 1981, Father died on April 6, the original date of the Last Supper.

At the time I asked Father about the Transforming Union, my knowledge about it was limited to the books I had read. From these, I had suspected he might be transformed because of the characteristics I found St. John of the Cross employed to illustrate the conduct of such persons. For example: not needing to remember appointments (for God Himself 'reminds' the person); reacting perfectly, although spontaneously, to diverse and unforeseen stimuli (because God Himself 'reacts' through the person); finding oneself strangely in the right place at the right time (because God Himself mysteriously arranges the person's daily events). On a psychological level, the interior operations remain imperceptible to the individual who lives in this transformed state. I observed in Father Aloysius's daily activity utterly amazing coincidences that begged for an explanation which "chance happening" seems unable to provide. It was as though everything had been planned in advance, even to the smallest details. I observed his behavior to be in complete harmony with external stimuli, for example, when he answered the telephone or encountered, at the very moment of leaving from or returning to the Provincial Residence, certain persons for whom the time of Father's presence would have seemed impossible to predict. It was as though a predetermined schedule was being followed without his knowing it. While I was overwhelmed by such incidents, he appeared virtually unaware of anything special. Any of these instances when taken isolatedly would not raise an eyebrow. But considered together the impression created was unmistakable—he was living under the Gifts of the Holy Spirit. Perhaps none of this drew Father's attention because he had already grown used to living this way (since 1940).

BEFORE LEAVING THE SUBJECT—and because this biography is meant to instruct our new seminarians—two clarifications seem in order. (1) Transforming Union is one thing, but the surrounding graces sensibly perceived on March 21, 1940, are something else. Normally, such a transformation takes place over a more or less lengthy period, immediately initiated by the Dark Night of the Spirit toward the end of the Sixth Mansion. The moment in which Transforming Union reaches its fullness normally is not distinguished by the person himself, but rather deduced from the powerful effects subsequently manifested in apostolic fruitfulness: "By their fruits you shall know them." For this reason, it is virtually impossible to point to a precise moment for the attainment of such fullness. Consequently, the graces Father Aloysius perceived while giving thanks at the foot of the tabernacle on Holy Thursday morning of 1940, were extraordinary. The word "extraordinary," when referring to special graces, refers to what is *extra* ("out of") the ordinary. Apparently the purpose of these graces was to verify to him the *fact* of having attained such an eminent stage in his spiritual development. Usually such knowledge—of where one is located on the path of holiness—is withheld from the soul. (2) In referring to Transforming Union as an "ordinary" grace, I wish to indicate that such a grace—no matter how uncommon or rare it may be in practice—is absolutely *normal* (as in 'normative') for anyone who perseveres on the road to sanctity. According to traditional spiritual masters, ordinary mystical graces should actually be desired, while the extraordinary mystical graces,[5] as externally perceptible charisms, should definitely not be desired.[6] The former should not only be desired, but the Saints would have us vehemently desire them, because they work powerfully to bring about the sanctity of the soul through the infused virtues that accompany them.[7]

---

[5] *The Graces of Interior Prayer* by Auguste Poulain, S.J., (St. Louis, MO: Herder, 1978[5]), pp. 457–58. The author uses different terminology: *exdéique* and *indéique*. What "exdéique" is for Poulain is "extraordinary" for our purposes. Only the terminology differs, but the same idea is affirmed.

[6] Vatican II teaches: "Extraordinary gifts are not to be sought after, nor are the fruits of apostolic labor to be presumptuously expected from their use" (*LG* 12). To desire such (as apparitions, locutions, etc.) is, according to St. John of the Cross, at least a venial sin (*Ascent*, II, 21, 4).

[7] St. Ignatius, in a letter to St. Francis Borgia (Rome, 1548), says: "All these very holy gifts should be preferred to all corporal acts, which are

Furthermore, ordinary mystical graces, since they remain interior and unseen, involve less risk of spiritual pride and vanity.[8] Since Father Aloysius was a teacher of the spiritual life, it appears suitable to his office that he, like St. Teresa of Avila, was made aware of the stages of the spiritual life

---

only good in so far as they serve to acquire these gifts, either wholly or in part. By this I do not mean to say that we should seek them solely for the pleasure and delectation that we find in them; certainly not. But recognizing that, without these gifts, all our thoughts, words, and works are imperfect, cold, and tarnished, we should desire these gifts in order that we may thereby become righteous, ardent, and bright, for God's greater service. It therefore follows that we should desire these most precious gifts, either wholly or in part, and these spiritual graces insofar as we can by their aid procure greater glory to God."

[8] Father advised people against going overboard about visions, apparitions, locutions, etc. While he himself was very devout in making the most of Church-approved apparitions, he discouraged people from curiously pursuing the neighborhood "mystics" and wasting time reading their "messages." (In my past forty years as a priest, I have seen several of these pseudo-mystics rise and fall in popularity, a few of whom were eventually censured by the Church as frauds. My advice to all faithful Catholics is to wait until the Church gives its full and final approval on these phenomena. I recommend reading Leon Christiani's *Evidence of Satan in the Modern World*, chapter 2, on how the devil appeared pretending to be the Blessed Mother, to numerous persons in Lourdes immediately following the true apparitions, in order to discredit the entire phenomenon; and my essay "Searching for a Sign," on line at our website: www.missionariesoffatima.org where I discuss Sister Magdalene of the Cross, in the 16th Century, who for 38 years had everyone convinced, including the hierarchy and great theologians, of her Satanic apparitions.) Perhaps Father Aloysius's favorite writer was Fr. Louis Lallemant, who said: "A well-disposed soul receives in a single Communion a favor greater beyond comparison than all that flows from all the visions and revelations which all the saints united have ever had" (*Spiritual Doctrine*, p. 233).

through which he passed, since such knowledge allowed him to educate others about the ways of interior prayer.

"How long does it take to receive such a grace?" I asked Father one day. His reply manifests his belief that this exalted grace is more "ordinary" than we usually suspect: "It would be fitting for a priest to receive this grace by the time he is ordained, because the priest is called to be another Christ."

"What is it that most prevents people from reaching such heights of sanctity?"

His answer was one word: "sensuality."[9] He meant self-indulgence, or a way of life in which gratification of the senses plays a major role, and penance very little or none.

"What should one do principally to receive this grace of transformation?"

He replied that the key virtue to hasten the reception of this most elevated grace is purity. He was referring to sexual purity which he considered the most difficult virtue for young men to acquire, because of the sacrifice it implies. Father's idea, as I recall, went as follows:

---

[9] Ignaz Watterott, whom I have had occasion to quote in chapter II, speaks of a veritable slavery of sensuality: "By sin man becomes his own slave... The evil appetite, once satisfied, becomes a desire and inclination; this in turn becomes a propensity and a passion; but this produces a man without a will, and binds him in fetters. Especially does this happen when sensuality is the object of the passion" (*Guidance of Religious*, 53–54).

The rejection of carnal desire, since it is the most difficult temptation to deny, is the fastest way to bring about complete detachment from anything that is not God. Experience proves that it involves the greatest humility, as it is a total sacrifice of the self. This lifts the soul to the greatest love of God possible on earth. At the moment of temptation, one should pray: "My dear God! I offer to you what is most difficult for me to reject—sexual pleasure. And I do it only for sheer love of you!"[10]

Father gave the above advice to young men and recommended natural and supernatural ways of overcoming temptation. Of capital importance was the mortification of the eyes for attaining not only mastery over the body but perfect peace of soul. "The eyes," he insisted, "are the floodgates of evil."

How much today's world, where pornography reigns supreme and ways of gratifying the senses abound, could benefit—if it comprehended these words! In a book that remained many years on the bestsellers list, the author explains that we have lost our freedom because we are unable to deny ourselves immediate gratification.[11]

---

[10] It may come as a surprise that purity should be given so much importance. Father was well aware of the remark of the Archbishop of Paris concerning the Jansenists of Port-Royal: "They are as pure as angels, but as proud as devils." However, this emphasis never led him to be inhuman about enjoying nature as a God-given motive for joy and recreation. Yet, having given spiritual advice for so many years, he fully realized how souls are easily attached to carnal appetite to the point of being incapable of denying themselves even in the case of mortal sin.

[11] Dr. M Scott Peck's *The Road Less Traveled* (New York: Simon & Schuster, 1978).

Left to ourselves, without God's grace to strengthen the will, there is only one alternative to self-denial: the total loss of freedom.[12] Hopefully we will wake up before it is too late.

---

[12] Watterott, in a statement which immediately follows his sentence quoted in our footnote (n. 9), gives that alternative: "Then man, even a priest and a religious, can fall so deep that the very thought fills us with horror. Whenever this passion has gained the upper hand over the better feelings and nobler sentiments of the heart, the cry of despair, 'I cannot help it any longer,' opens up a deep abyss of human misery and passion" (*Guidance of Religious*, 54).

V.

Apostolic Irradiation

Beginning in 1942, Father again was stationed in California teaching in Claretian seminaries, and specifically as prefect of studies for the philosophers. From 1948 to 1957 he was in Los Angeles at the Provincial House, as master of novices and spiritual moderator of twelve centers of Claretian Guilds in Los Angeles and its neighboring suburbs. He promoted devotion to the Immaculate Heart of Mary as symbolized by the white scapular. From 1952 until 1963, Father was local superior at the Provincial House on Westchester Place. Much of his time was spent visiting the sick and the dying. Remembering these fruitful years, Father wrote: "St. Anthony Mary Claret was then the most popular Saint among the sick whom I loved to visit and help in every way I could."[1]

In 1963, Father left California and was superior and pastor for three years in Phoenix, Arizona, at the Parish of the Immaculate Heart of Mary, and another three years (1966–69) in San Antonio, Texas, also at the Parish of the Immaculate Heart of Mary. In both cities Father received awards from the city councils for his beautification of the church buildings and the grounds around each church. He had a lively aesthetic sense together with very extensive knowledge about plants. Often when approaching a green area, he would pause and scrutinize each tree, bush, and flower. Taking a leaf between his fingers, he would identify

---

[1] Curriculum vitae.

each by its scientific name in Latin, explaining to anyone present its special characteristics.

Father looked upon those years in Phoenix and San Antonio as an "exile," caused ultimately by the excessive appeal of his healing ministry—sometimes bordering on fanaticism in some individuals. He, who had tried his best to avoid the limelight, was saddened that his apostolate to the sick and the dying had become a source of controversy. Although he resigned himself to any assignment outside of Los Angeles, he was not indifferent to the underlying causes in this case. By the time I met him (just after his return to Los Angeles and my return from the Peace Corps in Ethiopia) the Charismatic Renewal was in its initial boom. He confided to me: "Nowadays anyone imposes hands to pray over people. Only a few years ago you could be put away for doing that!"[2]

Returning from San Antonio, Texas, to Los Angeles Father remained stationed at the Provincial House from 1969 to 1971, after which he traveled to Fatima, Portugal, for the purpose of founding our congregation (1971–1973), which I will detail in chapter VI.

ONLY AFTER PASSING through the union which transforms a soul into another Christ, is the soul capable, like a torch, of irradiating the light of Christ everywhere. When speaking of "apostolic irradiation" what precisely do we expect to find? From what we have treated in our preceding two chapters, an evident difference exists between "activity" and "activism." The importance of *being* over *doing*—of prayer

---

[2] About this gesture, St. Augustine teaches: *Quid aliud est manuum imposition, quam oratio super hominem?* ("What else is the imposition of hands but prayer over a man?" [*De bapt.*, III, xvi, 21]).

over activity, of love over works—was the primary lesson to be learned from Father Aloysius's utter dependence on prayer. Soon after being elected, Pope St. John Paul II, echoing St. John of the Cross, made a statement that is unforgettable: "... A pause for true worship has greater value and spiritual fruit than the most intense activity, were it apostolic activity itself."[3] Pope St. Paul VI, in his final

---

[3] *L'Osservatore Romano*, English edition, Dec. 7, 1978, p. 3. (Cf. St. John of the Cross's *Spiritual Canticle*, Stanza 28, in the annotation for Stanza 29: "Therefore if any soul should have aught of this degree of solitary love, great wrong would be done to it, and to the Church, if, even but for a brief space, one should endeavor to busy it in active or outward affairs, of however great moment; for, since God adjures the creatures not to awaken the soul from this love, who shall dare to do so and shall not be rebuked? After all, it was to reach this goal of love that we were created" [...] "Let those, then, that are great actives, that think to girdle the world with their outward works and their preachings, take note here that they would bring far more profit to the Church and be far more pleasing to God (apart from the good example they would give of themselves) if they spent only half as much time in abiding with God in prayer, even had they not reached such a height as this. Of a surety they would accomplish more with one piece of work than they now do with a thousand, and that with less labor, since their prayer would be of such great deserving and they would have won such spiritual strength by it. For to act otherwise is to hammer vigorously and to accomplish little more than nothing, at times nothing at all; at times, indeed, it may even be to do harm" [Trans. E. Allison Peers]). The tendency to activism is already accepted as something normal. One of the best books on this subject is Josef Pieper's *Leisure the Basis of Culture* (Mentor Classics, 1952; reprinted in two new editions.) Considering the active life and the contemplative life, the best of both is the "mixed" life, which Our Lord chose for himself, because the active life, in this case, is the fruit of the contemplative life. For St. Teresa of Avila, the perfect harmonization of

discourse at the end of the Third Session of Vatican II, said: "The most important action a human being can perform is an act of contemplation." There is a famous story of St. Francis of Assisi, who was asked by one of the brothers, "What is the most important thing we must do as Christians?" Francis answered: "The most important thing we must do is preach the gospel; and if necessary, use words."

If apostolic irradiation begins more than anywhere else with one's presence—or from inside oneself where God lives—what did Father's presence manifests for those who approached him?

If you wished to consult Fr. Aloysius at the Provincial House in Los Angeles, you might find him seated behind his desk in full serenity; his hands are gently folded on his lap or on the desk in front of him. On the completely empty desk top, and to one side, is a beautiful blue and white alabaster statue of the Immaculate Conception. Father is smiling radiantly. After a brief glance, he gently closes his eyes, and listens attentively to your story. Whenever he speaks to you, his voice is marked by great effort to pronounce his words correctly. Even so, you make an effort to understand him on account of the Basque accent and because he is careful not to raise his voice.[4]

Martha and Mary comes with the cocoon experience of the Fifth Mansion. This is when active works begin to bear fruit.

[4] Basque was Father's first language, which he spoke exclusively until he was eleven. If we include Greek and Latin, English was Father's fifth language. I remember a woman at the guild meeting who chortled: "I cannot understand a word he is saying, but I just love it!" Father's "Basqueness" should not be ignored when one attempts to understand his character. It also may account for a great deal of the misunderstandings that surrounded his persona. J.J. Rousseau spoke of

Father thoroughly enjoys listening to and counseling penitents, as though nothing else remains on his heavy schedule. His response to some persons is an invitation to pray with him. In conversation with you, it all becomes part of a larger framework of constant prayer which constitutes the air he breathes. His advice is given with the utmost care not to hurt your feelings, which he always presumes are extremely delicate.[5]

Now you are kneeling in front of Father to receive his blessing before you leave. Father's body bears a very

---

the Basques as "our guest aliens in the household of Europe." In a language that falls completely outside the Indo-European trunk, and disconnected from any other world language, Father Aloysius was proud to be proficient in writing poetry. (Many Basques claim their language comes direct from Adam and Eve.) Father stated that if he had not left Spain when he did, he certainly would have been hunted down and killed in the Spanish Civil War because, in his words, he was "too Basque." On one occasion he begged us (his seminarians) to silence him if he ever again mentioned the glories of the Basque race, such as: (1) how the Romans were never able to conquer them; (2) the first man to go around the world was Basque (since Magellan was killed in the Philippines, his right-hand man, Juan Sebastian Elcano [†1526], completed the voyage and received from the King and Queen of Spain a golden orb with the words inscribed around it: *Tu primum me circumdedisti*); (3) several truly great Saints were Basques, including St. Ignatius of Loyola, St. Francis Xavier, St. Bernadette Soubirous, et alia.

[5] He understood himself so well and sometimes would say "I am so extremely sensitive; that is why I suffer so much [from contrarieties]." He concluded that others suffer the same plight, so he encouraged people to act and speak toward each other with the utmost care "... as though others were more sensitive than yourself."

delicate scent, suggestive of roses, and a perfectly pressed cassock still holds the fresh dryness from a hot iron. His entire person speaks of cleanliness, with that glowing quality I spoke of at the beginning of this book. The brilliance radiates from the unusual smoothness of his skin. There are no wrinkles on his face, even though he is over sixty-five years of age.

He is a little below average in height and a stocky build. The statue of St. Anthony Mary Claret in the chapel reminds you of him. In spite of his heavy build he walks with lightness and energy, the back straight and firm. As a young man he must have been a hardy athlete. In old age he remained very rugged, braving his daily duties with promptness and stoutheartedness.[6] The Basques in general are typically large boned with globe-like heads that appear larger than in other races.

In those years of apostolic irradiation, in spite of several times being afflicted with heart and circulatory problems, Father's resoluteness never wavered. In the final two years, he no longer walked vigorously, but supported himself with a cane after two hip replacements. Nevertheless, he continued to live the spiritual life as intensely as possible. In his efforts to help souls in their search for God, he would attend to their needs each day until reaching the point of complete exhaustion. When that moment arrived, he appeared almost drained of every drop of blood.[7]

---

[6] For many years he and some of the Claretian priests used to get up early in winter and swim in the cold ocean surf. They called themselves informally the "polar bear club."

[7] There are photographs from a pilgrimage to Jerusalem in 1975 which depict Father during the Stations of the Cross. He seems completely bled

Normally his day began at 6:00 a.m., with Lauds and meditation following at 6:30. He then would celebrate Holy Mass for the Sisters Servants of Mary, a few blocks south of the Provincial House, ten minutes away by car. Afterwards, he would attend to correspondence and telephone calls during the morning hours and received visits from persons asking for spiritual help. Priests liked to come to confession to him because of his great kindheartedness. He had a very high concept of the priesthood, no matter who the priest was. Once I saw a wayward priest enter his office. About an hour later, believing the visit had long before ended, I stumbled in to find the visiting priest standing before Father Aloysius, who was on his knees in suppliant attitude, as though he had been weeping. I have no idea what may have transpired. Nevertheless, shortly afterwards the wayward priest left the office with a bright, happy countenance.

ONE OF THE STRONGEST indications of unity with God is the power to attract vocations. Possibly no other Claretian priest attracted as many vocations as Father Aloysius. Young people, even hippies, were struck by his aura of holiness. Not one soul, no matter what kind of life previously led, was deemed by Father as beyond God's power to make a new, original Saint. Father liked to recall in his sermons an incident from the life of St. Bernard, who pleaded for the release of a malefactor who was being led to the gallows. The Saint took the convict to his monastery where the man persevered in religious life over thirty years

---

of his life forces and hardly able to stand up. Mr. Patrick Siefner is seen next to Father in the photographs and he said he didn't think Father was going to make it.

and died "in a most edifying manner."[8] Father's capacity to see in any person the greatest potential for sanctity was at times almost quixotic, but always exhilarating for those hearing their testimonies. We have seen how, whenever imposing hands on the heads of the sick, Father exhibited full confidence when he believed the cure was imminent. In a similar way, when instructing repentant sinners he always believed he was dealing with future saints. A few times, from the fickleness of the human will, this optimism would later on bring painful disappointment. But when anyone showed misgivings about *his* optimism, either in regard to the aptness of others or even of oneself, Father immediately remonstrated how we *never* are to underestimate the power of grace. In homilies he urged a complete oblivion about one's past: "You say you were such a big sinner? Well, that is what you once *were*... What you are *now* is all that matters. God only considers your present dispositions."

One day, perhaps five or six weeks after meeting Father, he asked whether I had ever thought of becoming a priest. My reply was an immediate Yes. I knew I was in good hands, so I had made up my mind previously that whatever he told me to do would be God's will. Always clear to me was that Father had a perfect respect for the personal freedom of those who consulted him.[9]

---

[8] Abbé Theodore Ratisbonne, *St. Bernard of Clairvaux* (Rockford, Illinois: Tan Books and Publishers, 1991) p. 93.

[9] Of course, if I could live my life again I would enter the seminary as early as possible. There's so much to learn and too little time to learn it. So, to any young man reading this who feels called to the priesthood, my advice is—the sooner you start the better. When speaking of the religious life in the *Summa Theologica*, St. Thomas Aquinas says that

WHEN FATHER ALOYSIUS eventually founded a new missionary community, the apostolate he recommended above all others to his followers was the spiritual attention to the sick and the dying. I was able to appreciate in depth his own apostolic zeal toward the sick and the dying when tragedy again hit my family six months after I had met Father. On April 27, 1970, my parents were driving north of Los Angeles when their car slipped off an ice-covered highway and lunged into a deep ravine on a slope once called the Grapevine. My mother agonized at the bottom of the ravine and died before an ambulance arrived. My father, very seriously wounded, took another seven weeks to die.

News quickly spread. In a few hours Father Aloysius called me to give his condolences. His tenderness in expressing his own grief is incredible. He, who never lingered on a woman's face, began telling me how impressed he had been the evening before with my mother's eyes. He repeated several times: "I can still see her eyes!" The previous night we, as a family, had attended the annual Claretian "Musicale" in the Knollwood Country Club of Northridge, at which my eldest sister had sung arias and light classical favorites. Next day, when I reached the Kern County Hospital in Bakersfield, a nurse handed me the scapular medal Father Aloysius had personally blessed for my mother and which she was wearing at the moment of her death. This provided me with untold consolation.

My father eventually died from an undiscovered occlusion on his brain. On that day, June 15, 1970, Father Aloysius, who had previously anointed my father many

---

once you *know* you are called, it's a mistake even to consult others; one must respond to Christ's call immediately.

times, arrived approximately fifteen minutes after clinical death. Everyone had already left my father's body where it lay in a small cubicle in intensive care. Father wanted to see the deceased body. I took him into the room. He placed his hand on my father's chest and said, "Feel this! Your father is still very much alive! The soul has not yet departed from the body. Only a few moments remain before he will be judged. Let us say the fifteen decades of the Holy Rosary for him during this turbulent battle with the devil." We recited the Holy Rosary together, which was the greatest consolation to me, and undoubtedly much more than that for my father.

During the tragic weeks of that spring in 1970, I was buoyed along by God's grace. Father Aloysius helped me to see life in an entirely new manner. During my father's funeral, Father Aloysius, upon seeing my youngest siblings, wept more profusely than anyone else. In all things he taught others to see better and more clearly through the eyes of faith. I was impressed by his observations even about everyday matters, turning what otherwise escapes our attention into spiritual gold. Hardly could this manner of seeing not rub off on those who knew Father, in spite of our slowness in understanding things in a spiritual way.

How was Father able to accompany countless other people through their trials and sufferings? Today many people tell me they are amazed he was able to recognize each one's voice on the phone, as well as remember everyone's names in their families. He could not be physically present as often as he would have wished, but each one of us remained in his heart.

Whatever this was, today it reminds me of the friendship between Christ and St. John the Evangelist at the Last Supper. In that hour, St. John received the mysterious understanding of the love that lay hidden in the Sacred Heart of Jesus. Father, as a man transformed by Christ living in him, went through life sharing his Eucharistic love with others.

VI.

Founder

A pilgrimage to Europe was scheduled for October, 1970. As chaplain, Father Aloysius managed to include me on the trip. From the three weeks overseas, three events stand out in my mind which point to the founding of his new religious community.

The first was the Holy Mass which was celebrated in the Cistercian monastery of Fontfroide, France. This Mass was held in the same place, and on the centenary, of the death of St. Anthony Mary Claret, October 24, 1870. The Mass, which I had the privilege of serving as acolyte, was scheduled so that the consecration would occur at 8:30 a.m., the very moment of St. Anthony's death one hundred years earlier. Something definitely special was reenacted for all of us. It only became clear to me when Father wrote the reasons why he wanted to found a house of prayer for the Claretian Congregation—to fulfill St. Anthony Mary Claret's own wishes.

The second event took place a few days later in Lourdes. We pilgrims arrived late at night and were assigned to several rooms in a hotel. The next morning, two young men were telling me how they had spent the entire night discussing monastery buildings. One of them was a son of an engineer and both had sat in the middle of the floor making huge drawings of how the "ideal" monastery should look.[1] Among many details that overflowed from their explanations, one in particular was emphasized: the perfect

---

[1] The two young men were Jim Smith and Craig Bowditch.

monastery must have, right at the very center, a chapel for Eucharistic Adoration.

Outside the hotel on that brisk morning, Father Aloysius stood surrounded by a small group of our pilgrims. The two young men enthusiastically told Father what was on their minds. Then they asked, "Father, have you ever thought of building a monastery?" "Of course," he immediately replied. Father's statement surprised me. Never before had I heard him mention such a dream.

The third event was our visit to Fatima on November 1 and 2. Father approached the provincial superior of the Portuguese Claretians and presented to him the idea of bringing a group of young men to Fatima to start a special project for a house of prayer, specifically of perpetual Eucharistic adoration. The superior, very impressed with the idea, gave his consent, saying that the novitiate had only sixteen novices, when there was room for fifty. When Father had good ideas, he wanted as soon as possible to see them a reality.

Back in Los Angeles, Father Aloysius continued corresponding with the provincial superior of Portugal about this inspiration. Since this project concerned two Claretian provinces, he deemed it prudent to present his ideas to the Superior General at the end of May, 1971, when the General was to visit Los Angeles. Meanwhile, Father Aloysius suggested to some of the young men who used to come to him for spiritual counseling the possibility of their joining this group.

What precisely was Father's original idea? Certainly it was not to reform his own order, nor to found a new order. Father explained that it had been St. Anthony Mary Claret's desire that in each Province of the Claretian Congregation there be a house dedicated exclusively to Perpetual Adoration. Since a hundred years had passed and this desire had never materialized, it appeared to Father the appropriate moment to launch the plan, as a "gift to the Immaculate Heart of Mary," had arrived. And, no place seemed more fitting than Fatima, because of the Eucharistic-Cordimarian aspect of the message of Fatima.

When the Superior General, Fr. Antonio Leghisa, CMF, arrived in Los Angeles in the spring of 1971, Father Aloysius spoke to him in person on May 24, and received his approval. Four days later Father Aloysius presented to him a letter to ratify the interview. The letter explains Father Aloysius's plan as "The possibility of establishing Perpetual Adoration in Fatima as a tribute on the Centennial of the death of St. Anthony Mary Claret who was the living monstrance of the Most Blessed Sacrament." The Superior General read the letter and returned it a few hours later with a note in his own handwriting at the bottom: "Le doy mi permiso con mucho gusto" (*I give you my permission with great pleasure*), together with his signature and the date (May 28, 1971).

Over the following months, Father Aloysius was in contact with six or seven young men willing to join the project. One day, while dictating a letter concerning the same, and apparently as an afterthought, he interrupted himself to ask me, "Would you like to become a part of this group?" Immediately as I answered Yes, he stood up and came around the desk toward me. I knelt to receive his blessing. For a long time his hands remained firmly on my head; meanwhile I felt something like a heavy rainfall upon me. At a distance of almost 50 years, it seems God was granting me the grace to persevere in the congregation.

Approximately three times a month, the young men invited by Father would meet with him on a Sunday afternoon at the home of some of his friends. On several occasions we met at Mr. and Mrs. Ted Flocca's house in La

Crescenta. This nice elderly couple did not know the purpose of these visits, but generously opened their home and served us a delicious meal when the meetings ended in the late afternoon. The first two or three times I attended, no one took notes. Then Father told me in emphatic terms, "Do take notes. They will be very important in the future." I kept notes, which extend from that summer into the fall, and continue into our novitiate in Fatima, Portugal, which began in October, 1971. Because these notes do not contain the first two or three meetings, the first day to appear is July 31, 1971. And the first words, evidently at the middle of an explanation, are: "Positively NEVER any television."

On October 9, 1971, ten young men together with Father Aloysius flew from Los Angeles to London on a charter flight for $110.00 each. From there we immediately flew to Lisbon, arriving late at night on October 11. We managed to cram ourselves and the baggage into two taxis from Lisbon to Fatima. Ringing the doorbell at the Claretian Seminary at 3:00 AM brought no results, so we spent the rest of the night at the Shrine. We warmed ourselves at the large grated pit, loaded with huge lighted candles, which represents the shepherd children's "Vision of Hell" (July 13, 1917). In the morning, the Claretians were all apologies. Yes, they had gone to the airport for us. But with the ten-hour delay of our flight they had returned downhearted to Fatima a few hours before our arrival. We were shown around the house and soon felt at home.

A few days later, the provincial superior arrived from Lisbon and indicated that we should use the older chapel for our community prayers, leaving the larger chapel for the sixteen Portuguese novices. Likewise, we were allowed to occupy one floor of bedrooms, the Portuguese novices another. We got along well with the Portuguese novices who averaged about five years younger than us. We took meals and played soccer with them and they helped us learn Portuguese.

For the next two months our life in the novitiate was normal. Father gave us conferences each day: first, an in-depth treatise on abiding sorrow,[2] the firmest foundation of the spiritual life, which took several days to explain; then the meaning of religious vows. Digressions, usually on fascinating examples from the lives of the saints, abounded. Father celebrated Mass for us each day at noon; whenever possible this was done at the "Little Chapel of the Apparitions." Every evening we had Holy Hour before the exposed Blessed Sacrament in our chapel from 8:00 to 9:00 p.m. Total prayer time in the chapel was three hours a day.

A visit to Fatima by Arcadio Cardinal Larraona, CMF, (†1973) was a highlight. We greeted him in front of the Claretian novitiate and, without any other words preceding or following this brief encounter, he asked, "Are you carrying a cross?" We gazed at him in silence. He added, "That is the *only* way we know we are doing God's will." Then he walked away.

On December 7, 1971, the Bishop of Leiria-Fatima, João Pereira Venâncio, came to Fatima and invested us in our habits (a black cassock and sash) in the novitiate chapel.

---

[2] The concept of "abiding sorrow" (πένθος) was well elaborated among the Greek Fathers of the Church. It continues to be considered by many the enduring root of the conversion that attains final perseverance. See F.W. Faber's chapter "Abiding Sorrow for Sin," in *Growth in Holiness* (Westminster, MD: The Newman Press, 1960). In the context of our novitiate, Father Aloysius began by explaining the process of purification given by St. Ignatius in the first week of the *Spiritual Exercises*.

In his homily he encouraged us with the unforgettable words: "Any work that begins in Fatima will never fail."

Four days later, on December 11, 1971, Father Aloysius became very ill and had to be transferred out of the novitiate to the home of some recently-made friends. The name of the house was *A Casa da Azinheira* (The House of the Holm Oak Tree). He recuperated there for four months until April 15, 1972, when he moved back into our community. During Father's absence we visited him daily as a group to continue his novitiate instructions and attend Mass which he celebrated for us privately.

On February 1, 1972, unexpected by us, the Claretian Superior General arrived from Rome at the Novitiate in Fatima. He spoke privately first with the Portuguese superiors and then alone with Father Aloysius. That evening, after the General's departure, Father Aloysius spoke to us (his novices) at the home where he was recuperating. He explained the purpose of Father General's visit. The Father General was inviting us to form a religious community directly dependent on the General Government of the Claretian Congregation. (As mentioned in the letter shown below, the Superior General's original plan was vetoed a week later by his Council.) Father Aloysius's attitude was very grave. In brief, we were invited to be loyal to Father Aloysius in a split that would inevitably take place. I remember Father asking me directly, in front of the others, if I was going to be a coward and back down. The question was embarrassing and I was glad to affirm my adherence to him and to the group.[3]

---

[3] As I have mentioned in chapter Five, Father respected each one's freedom to make an initial choice. But when it was a question of seminarians wavering when things got difficult, he was extremely tenacious in his struggle against their abandoning religious life.

Approximately two weeks later a letter, dated February 9, 1972, came to the Novitiate for Father Aloysius from the Superior General. This letter was forever after accepted by Father Aloysius as an order to be followed from obedience. The contents were immediately considered by him as the foundation of our Congregation. The following is a translation.

Rome, February 9, 1972

Dear Father Aloysius,

This letter is to reply to the petitions you made to me in Fatima and which I brought with me to Rome for you. I do not know if I have been a good lawyer. One thing is certain: the solution we are giving you has many advantages and avoids many inconveniences. At any rate, let us permit Divine Providence to act.

Here is what our General Government, in its advisory session on February 7, has decreed, after studying all the information at our disposal:

(1) The group of young Americans at present novices in our novitiate in Fatima follows aims and methods which, although good, are not compatible with the aims and methods of our Congregation;

(2) For the same reason, the group of young Americans will have to separate from the Portuguese group, even in regard to lodging. Your Reverence together with the Provincial Superior can arrange upon the time and the manner of effectuating this move.

(3) The group constituted by Your Reverence must be considered as a new foundation. At present we cannot recognize it or classify it among the Claretian works, properly speaking. Your Reverence also must look for another name, not Claretian, for the group.

(4) In a letter dated today I am writing to the Bishop of Leiria-Fatima and I am recommending that he erect the new foundation, first as an association recognized by him and

then as a diocesan institute, as Your Reverence expresses in the letter which you gave me. Thus, we follow Canon Law and the practice of the Church.

(5) In order to determine your personal situation, you can reach an agreement with your Provincial Superior, Father Bernard O'Connor, CMF, so that he obtains for you a permission to remain outside your community for a period of one to three years, naturally without your ceasing to be a Claretian. I assume the Bishop will happily give you his Nihil Obstat. I am writing favorably to Fr. O'Connor.

(6) Father Palacín, the Provincial Superior of Cantabria, will pass through Fatima on his trip to Bolivia, to see if he can help you in some way.

I believe the solution we are giving you is more positive than negative. What matters is that you, just as you have done with the Sisters, do not be afraid likewise to take an autonomous path with the group of students, if the Church recognizes it through the Bishop.

Since we are on the subject, note that the name of the Sisters which Your Reverence founded is used by another religious Congregation already approved by the Church. When your Congregation is approved by the Church they will oblige you to change the title. It is better to effect the change right away with some variant, by adding on or taking off a word.

Taking the opportunity to greet you warmly, in Corde Matris,

[Signed] Fr. Antonio Leghisa, CMF

[PS] I suppose your health is improving. We pray that such be the case. Greetings to the young men there with you.

The date of the letter, February 9, 1972, automatically became our founding date and to this day we celebrate it as such. By removing "Claretian" as the first word from our title, our name became: "Missionaries of

Perpetual Adoration."[4] Some of the letter's content may appear puzzling to the reader. For example, what does "religious Sisters" refer to? This and other details will become clearer as we continue our story.

On February 15 our community of seminarians moved out of the Claretian Novitiate and into a large unoccupied building called the Casa of St. John Eudes. This building was still under construction at the time and is perched on a hill above the olive groves behind the Blue Army's Domus Pacis. The charitable Sisters of St. John Eudes rented us this three-storey building with its unpainted cement interior. On April 15, the weather being more clement, Fr. Aloysius came from the house where he had been recuperating to live with us.

Although we effectively separated from the Portuguese community, our fond memories of them remained firmly rooted in our hearts. When asked by the Claretian community "What do you think of the Portuguese character?" Father replied: "I am deeply impressed by the Portuguese, by their deep faith, great simplicity, much goodness, and special love for the Blessed Mother. They are hardy and able to withstand much privation. They are tremendously thrifty, transforming rocks into bread."[5]

During that spring, Fr. Aloysius and I approached the Bishop of Leiria-Fatima to comply with Fr. General's

---

[4] The original title "Missionaries of Perpetual Adoration," although still official for internal religious purposes, is no longer used by us in the civil domain. We changed our legal title in 1989 to "Missionaries of Fatima," primarily to provide tax deductions for our benefactors.

[5] Written questionnaire (October 19, 1971) submitted to Father Aloysius by the Portuguese Claretians. We will have further occasion to speak of this questionnaire.

expressed wish. The Bishop's attitude was promising. He invited Father to present the statutes of our proposed institute. Statutes are not exactly the same as constitutions, but are more simplified, amounting to an outline on the nature of the institute, its aims, means, and basic norms.

Shortly afterward, Fr. Aloysius made a trip to Madrid to ask a canon lawyer to take on the task of composing the rules for our nascent institute, based on Father's inspiration as founder. The person Father chose was Fr. Timoteo de Urkiri, CMF, a Basque priest and expert in writing constitutions for religious orders according to the norms for renewal as expressed in Vatican II's *Perfectae Caritatis*. Father de Urkiri was most willing to help out. Nevertheless, more than six years passed before our Constitutions saw the light of day in September, 1978.

Meanwhile we were left without a rule of life, virtually incapable of satisfying the legitimate demands of the Bishop. The Bishop most probably would have given us an initial written approval as a Public Association of the Faithful, since he had already done such a favor for the religious Sisters founded by Fr. Aloysius. As we have already observed, the Superior General in his letter of February 9 refers to a community of Sisters. Who are these Sisters?

In the first and second chapter I mentioned a very gifted nun from France coming to Los Angeles in 1970. During her visit, plans were envisioned to set up one of her communities in the United States.[6] When the plan failed, there remained a few women gathered around Father Aloysius with desires to enter the would-be French

---

[6] Her Congregation was called "Les Petites Servantes du Christ-Roi" (*Little Handmaids of Christ the King*).

community in the States. Instead of letting them down, Father told them to wait. A few of these women soon joined Mother Marguerite Carter in Fallbrook, California, in her active Carmelite community, a foundation in which Fr. Aloysius also had been instrumental many years earlier. Finally, Father thought of founding another community of Sisters with a Claretian spirituality. The idea actually originated a few months previous to initiating our own community of men. The sisters would be called "The Missionary Daughters of St. Anthony Mary Claret." This is the name the Claretian Superior General objected to later on, for the simple reason that a Claretian Bishop (of Londrina, Brazil) had already founded years earlier an order of nuns with the same name. When Father Aloysius arrived in Fatima in 1971, he immediately asked the Bishop to approve this new group of Sisters, still in its initial formation stages in Los Angeles, which he planned to bring to Fatima to establish their motherhouse. The Bishop generously drew up a decree approving this new group of Sisters, dated January 26, 1972. We needed to locate a home for them and happily settled on the *Casa da Azinheira*, since the owners wished to sell. This is the same place, it will be remembered, in which Father convalesced from December 11, 1971 to April 15, 1972. The new Sisters eventually arrived in May of 1972. As the title indicates, the Sisters were not a feminine branch of our order. Most unfortunately, they disbanded sometime in 1974, not long after Father Aloysius returned to the United States. Their presence in Fatima will always remain in our hearts as well-remembered friends, and a reminder of what would have happened to our own group—even more easily, since we did not have a Bishop's written approval—had God not extended an incredible protection over us.

Why found a new order?

While giving external events in the history of our Institute, it may be helpful to answer a question: If there are so many orders in the Church, why found another one? It is true that the Fourth Lateran Council (1215) prohibited the founding of new orders. But this refers to *orders* with a new set of rules. Since that time, innumerable *congregations* have been founded, always basing their rule on one of the ancient orders.

More precisely, what were Father Aloysius's intentions? The Portuguese superiors at the Novitiate asked Father Aloysius to give his opinion about his motives in starting our community in Fatima. Even though he was not yet contemplating founding a new (i.e., separate) congregation, his reply to their seven questions were written down, and merit attention. The sixth question here follows with a reply that is quite revealing:

Q. What do you think of the present crisis in the church?

A. The present crisis in the church is a result of a lack of proper spiritual formation in the seminaries, and because of that, priests today are not as they should be. This crisis is going to be much worse because, in the present day the seminaries, instead of being improved, are completely deteriorated, and the ones in charge of sacerdotal formation, sad to say but it is a fact, are the instruments of deformation of the future priests. "The priest, by virtue of his vocation," in the expression of St. John Eudes, "is called to the highest dignity on earth, and therefore to the highest sanctity." This great Saint and a great director of seminaries in his day used to state this maxim many, many times to the seminarians and priests in his conferences or spiritual retreats. I stated that the crisis is going to be much worse because, since the Council of Trent, the seminaries have never been so corrupted as in the present day. Pardon my expression, but this happens to be true. In most of the seminaries they have a disastrous misinterpretation of Vatican II, and I state this with all my conviction, after spending twenty-five years or more in the spiritual formation of seminarians. As a house, to weather the storms, should have solid foundations and then be properly built, likewise the seminarians, as future priests, should have a thorough and deep foundation in the *purgative life* which most of them don't have, and then be led into the *illuminative life* by the most expert and holy spiritual directors of the diocese or congregation, and by the time of their ordination they should be entering fully the *unitive life,* because the priest is another Christ and should be *one with Christ,* not only in name but in deed.

When they asked him, "Why in Fatima?" Father inserted the three reasons he had written to his Superior General on September 13, 1970, and then added a fourth:

"I thought that the best place for this should be in Fatima for several reasons:

1. It was the Angel of Portugal in 1916 who brought to Lucia, Jacinta, and Francisco, to adore and receive under both species, the Most Blessed Sacrament;
2. Because Fatima, since 1917, has been and is considered the holiest place in the world;
3. Because our dear Father Founder, St. Anthony Mary Claret, has been promoted by the Bishop of Leiria-Fatima, to be the patron and Generalissimo-in-chief of the Blue Army of Our Lady of Fatima, that counts over 20 million people over the world. And Fatima is the international headquarters of this holy organization." And it is noteworthy that
4. St. Anthony Mary Claret was proclaimed by his Holiness Pius XII, the Forerunner of Fatima. In January, 1971, I published an article in *Soul* magazine stating twelve reasons why St. Anthony Mary Claret is a perfect prophet and forerunner of Fatima and of its entire message.

Later on in the following year, Father wrote a letter to future members of the "Missionaries of Perpetual Adoration," in which he states what appears to support the need for a new congregation:

> I want only those to join this Congregation who are determined to become saints and to deny themselves for pure love of God, and to wage war always against the devil, the flesh and the world. God wants that this be an order of saints, and eventually quite a few of them will be martyrs for their faith in and their love for the Eucharistic Christ. Even those who have been sinners can become saints by regretting thoroughly their sins and offering Christ an ardent, repentant love. I don't want any mediocres here. Only sincerely good people who wish to spend their lives thoroughly in God's service in prayer and penance, and real zeal for the salvation of souls, particularly for those in their last agony.[7]

Regardless of Father's attitudes about religious life in today's secularized atmosphere, he never considered himself to have founded our Congregation, at least on his own initiative. In a letter to me, dated May 29, 1978, Father, when speaking about the new Congregation, says:

> I must make the sacrifice of being completely away from this Congregation which was founded not by me, but by the orders of my Father General when we were in Fatima, the letter which I received on February 9, 1972, telling me to start a new Congregation and this Congregation, he added, should not have any Claretian name or affiliation with the Claretians. So, it should be completely independent. It was

---

[7] Dated May 4, 1972, on our letterhead stationery of Fatima, Portugal. This letter, although dictated to me by Father Aloysius and carrying his name, remained unsigned and unmailed.

not my will, it was the orders of Almighty God through my Superior General of the Claretian Congregation of which I am most happily an obedient member.

FATHER REMAINED A MEMBER of the Claretian Congregation until death. He founded our order *ad extra*, that is, as a work outside the jurisdiction of his own order, even though that was not his original intention, as we observed above. About the possibility of leaving the Claretian Congregation there was no doubt in his own mind. He used to recall the promise of St. Anthony Mary Claret: "No one who dies within the Claretian Congregation will be condemned." In essence, Father would not risk his own salvation. As far as we young men were concerned, the likelihood of forfeiting such an advantage would seem remote as we had never formally entered the Claretians (i.e., by vows).

Once the 'split'—the word is used in a non-strict sense—was effected, Father remained, in a certain understanding, invested by his Superior General to do the work of a founder. In some of the correspondence he received from his Superior General, it is clear that permission of subaltern superiors is needed. Prior to the split, that of the provincial superior of Portugal and of the Western Province of the United States (seat in Los Angeles) were obtained.[8] After the separation, the permission of the

---

[8] These permissions were obtained in a timely fashion: See letters from Fr. João de Freitas Alves, CMF, Provincial Superior of Portugal, dated September 8, 1971, and of September 29, 1971. On his part, Fr. Bernard O'Connor, CMF, Provincial Superior in Los Angeles, writes on January 21, 1972 (before the separation): "You have whatever permission is required for your stay," and on September 7, 1972 (after the separation): "Father Aloysius Ellacuria, CMF, is a member in good standing of the Claretians of the Western Province... Fr. Ellacuria has recently been on a special assignment in Fatima, Portugal, the founding

Provincial Superior in Los Angeles was sufficient. Throughout the following years, the Superior General ever remained endeared to our work, and his letters are seasoned with brief but encouraging remarks, of which the following give evidence (the second of which has already been quoted):

October 3, 1971: "Father, I am not opposed to your projects. I told you this already in person."

February 9, 1972: "One thing is certain: the solution we are giving you has many advantages"... "Let us allow Divine Providence to act"... "I suppose the Bishop will happily give his Nihil Obstat"... "I believe the solution we are giving you is more positive than negative."

May 27, 1972: "I wrote to the Bishop some months ago, when I recommended your work to him."

November 21, 1972: "I regret that Bishop Venâncio has not responded to my letter of February 9 in which I support you and your work and in which I recommend him to do as much"... "I am writing now to the new Bishop in the sense in which Your Reverence has indicated to me"... "I extend to you my best wishes in favor of your works."

January 13, 1973: "God willing, may the works you have instituted receive during this New Year a greater dynamism and be strengthened in vocations and formation."... "Our General Secretary by this time has already communicated to you or to Father O'Connor the permission to stay out of the community with the aim of furthering those works."

---

or establishing in Portugal of a Congregation of men of Perpetual Adoration, which has no relation or connection with the Claretian Congregation. Fr. Ellacuria has been given permission for this work by our Superior General in Rome."

January 26, 1973: "It is my desire that all things be arranged, even juridically, so that an activity that can bring benefit to the Church not be lost or become less effective. If some difficulty arises, it is from the desire to keep within the legislation of the Church. But God has recourses we are unaware of. Let us abandon ourselves to the goodness of his Divine Will. And the future will be the guaranty of the present, which at times is so difficult and dark."

May 23, 1973: "You know that I always supported you. And, I only went back because the Bishop of Leiria-Fatima thus demanded it from me."

Aims of the Congregation

What inspiration, if any, did Father Aloysius receive regarding this congregation? As I mentioned in Chapter IV, the second reason why Holy Thursday was important in the life of Father Aloysius concerned the founding of our Congregation. During Holy Week in 1972, all of us attended the liturgical services together in the Basilica in Fatima. Because of Father's weakened health, he did not concelebrate, but remained with us in the back pews. After the Thursday ceremony, he told us he had received a very strong inspiration during the liturgy concerning our Congregation. As we listened to him on the steps of the Basilica, we were deeply impressed by what appeared to be a most unique, illuminating moment in Father's life. Overpowered by the experience, Father described the aims of our Congregation. Although I never will forget his words nor the great conviction with which he spoke of the experience, it did not appear he was referring to an apparition or a locution. An almost identical experience occurred the following day. I prefer to quote his written words from a letter he wrote to me six years later concerning the event:

> In regard to your suggestion for the Holy Constitutions, I will tell you briefly the aims of the new Congregation of Missionaries of Perpetual Adoration of the Most Blessed Sacrament and Perpetual Veneration of the Immaculate Heart of Mary.
>
> As I was in the Basilica of Fatima during the services on Holy Thursday and Good Friday, in 1972, I felt very strongly, very strongly, the inspiration that the new Congregation... should be a living Holy Thursday all their lives, by imitating St. John the Evangelist in his dearest love for our Sacramental Lord, as he was resting his head on the Holy Breast of Jesus.
>
> And, on Good Friday I felt likewise a strong inspiration that the Missionaries of Perpetual Adoration... should be a living Good Friday, particularly as Our Lord was hanging on the cross and looking at His Blessed Mother and told her, "Behold thy son," and then looking at St. John, told him, "Behold thy Mother," and nevermore did St. John leave the Blessed Mother.
>
> He was always with the Blessed Mother. He always bestowed every attention with all devotion to the Blessed Mother, in the same way the Missionaries of Perpetual Adoration... should live constantly the words, "Behold thy Mother," first the address to the Blessed Mother, then the address to St. John.
>
> The Holy Gospel says that forevermore St. John took Her into his own. Finally, St. John built in Ephesus a house for the Blessed Mother, and there the Blessed Mother died, surrounded by all the Apostles, particularly attended by the special love of St. John. The Blessed Mother was the Mother of the Church. The Mother of the Apostles, particularly the Mother of St. John. Likewise, the Immaculate Heart will be the most special Mother of the Missionaries of Perpetual Adoration of the Most Blessed Sacrament and Perpetual Veneration of the Immaculate Heart of Mary. So the new Congregation should be a living Holy Thursday and a living

Good Friday in their love for the Blessed Sacrament, in their filial love for the Immaculate Heart of Mary.

This is to emulate St. John the Evangelist who appears on the escutcheon of the Missionaries of Perpetual Adoration... St. John appears as an eagle protecting his new Congregation, that will be strong and most potent in the last period of the world. We are approaching that last period, we are already in the eschatological age. We are already under the prophecy of the twelfth chapter of the Apocalypse of St. John the Evangelist as has been announced publicly by eminent Churchmen speaking to assemblies of priests.

The Missionaries of Perpetual Adoration... will fight under the special protection of and safeguarded by the Immaculate Heart of Mary who announced at Fatima: "At the end my Immaculate Heart will triumph."[9]

---

[9] Letter of May 29, 1978.

VII.

Leavetaking

Shortly after Father General's letter of February 9, 1972, Father Aloysius, following the instructions outlined therein, approached the Bishop of Leiria-Fatima, His Excellency, João Pereira Venâncio. The Bishop gave us a warm welcome. After we explained the purpose of our visit, the Bishop asked us why the Superior General, who had traveled to Fatima just previously, had not visited the Bishop if he had something so important to communicate. We explained that the idea of a new foundation only arose after the Father General's return to Rome. The Bishop concurred with the idea and asked Father Aloysius to prepare statutes to present to him. As mentioned in our previous chapter, Father Aloysius had recourse to an expert in drawing up constitutions for religious orders—Father Timoteo de Urkiri, CMF—during a short visit to Spain in the spring of 1972. The project of statutes would grow into full-blown Constitutions taking over five years to complete.

Unfortunately, and unannounced to anyone, João, the Bishop of Leiria, resigned on August 15, 1972. Bishop João had been well disposed toward us. We had looked forward to receiving, as soon as statutes could be presented, some initial approval, similar to what he so generously had granted to the Sisters.

Thus, the following February, we approached the new bishop, his Excellency Cosme do Amaral, to repeat the request we had made to his predecessor for acceptance as a new religious community. Together with Mother Claret Claire Ritchot (the Mother Superior of the Missionary Daughters), I accompanied Father Aloysius to the Bishop's offices in the medieval city of Leiria, about half an hour down the hill from Fatima. The Bishop, an extremely grave and reserved man, member of the Opus Dei, appeared to be uncomfortable with this new project, especially since there were so many religious orders in Fatima. The Bishop did not speak directly about rejecting the community, but we perceived a colder and far less enthusiastic attitude than we had hoped to find in him. Father Aloysius, reacting out of apprehension, immediately placed the entire matter in the hands of the Bishop and the Superior General. He did this by explaining that the latter truly was the "Founder" because, after all, it was the Superior General who had told him to approach the Bishop with this request; the Bishop, therefore, should communicate with the Superior General whatever the Bishop might decide. Apparently Father felt he stood a better chance by raising the matter to the level of giants. (And, above all, he would be spared receiving a negative directly from the Bishop.) The meeting was over in ten minutes.

On March 21, 1973, a letter arrived from the Superior General with an enclosed copy of a letter (dated March 1, 1973) from the new Bishop of Leiria-Fatima. In his letter, the Superior General explains to Father Aloysius the negative results of his own appeal to the Bishop. The Bishop, in his correspondence, refuses the request and asks the Superior General to implement our retreat from Fatima as soon as possible. Father Aloysius's reaction was one of shock and profound sadness.

The next morning it appeared Father had hardly slept during the night. At breakfast we always read from the *Imitation of Christ*. It was Brother Richard Konen's turn to read.[1] Since no one but Father and I knew about the letter from Rome and its fateful contents, the reading could not have been purposely chosen, that is, with an eye to mitigating the sad news received the previous day. Nonetheless, the reading could not have been better suited in the circumstances. It was Book III, chapter 29, filled with consoling words about the man upon whom a most unbearable suffering has suddenly and unexpectedly descended:

> Blessed, oh Lord, be Thy name forever, who hast been pleased that this trial and tribulation should come upon me. —*Dan.* 3:26.
>
> I cannot fly from it, but must of necessity fly to Thee that Thou mayest help me, and turn it to my good.
>
> Lord, I am now in tribulation, and my heart is not at ease; but I am much afflicted with my present suffering.

---

[1] Richard Konen was with our group in Fatima from September, 1972, until we disbanded in 1973. He eventually became a priest in 1976 for the Diocese of Ciudad Obregon, Sonora, and as such he preceded us into Mexico, where he spoke to the Bishop about us. He died on December 20, 2013, in Navojoa, Sonora, in the Lourdes Hospital.

And now, dear Father, what shall I say? I am caught, oh Lord, in straitened circumstances: Oh save me from this hour. —*Jn.* 12:27.

But for this reason I came unto this hour, that Thou mightst be glorified when I shall be exceedingly humbled and delivered by Thee.[2]

When referring to the great trials of the spiritual life, Father used the word *dereliction* to describe utter abandonment by God and others. For me this particular word says it all. From the arrival of the letters onward, Father Aloysius seemed never to emerge from a profound state of grief and sorrow, at least not before our departure from Fatima on August 1, 1973. He remained for the most part in his room on the second floor of St. John Eudes' guesthouse. To add to the problem, someone falsely accused him to the Bishop of having visited the site of an unapproved apparition several miles from Fatima. Coupled with the many and great moral sufferings typical of founders was his heart condition. His anguish often caused his blood pressure to rise dangerously, and he feared having another heart attack. During Holy Thursday ceremonies in the Basilica that spring, he did not have the strength to concelebrate the Mass with the other priests. He remained in the back pews. I recall him after the ceremonies sitting down from exhaustion on the front steps of the Basilica, supporting his head with one hand. No one stopped to greet him.

---

[2] Thomas à Kempis, *My Imitation of Christ* (Brooklyn, NY: Confraternity of the Precious Blood, 1954), p. 259.

One evening during Holy Hour, I was called from the chapel to find Father Luis Kondor, SVD, arriving to inform us about some aspect of his apostolate. This devout and energetic priest from Hungary, who worked as Vice-Postulator in an office in Fatima specially dedicated to furthering the causes for the beatification of Francisco and Jacinta Marto, had become over the past months a good friend of our group. I seized the opportunity to tell him about Father Aloysius's health and that we were already making plans to leave Fatima. I was surprised to learn that Father Kondor knew nothing about the Bishop's dispositions toward our community. Fr. Kondor almost daily had business to take care of at the Diocesan curia and was on very good terms with the Bishop. His disbelief about the Bishop's disposition led him to ask me to see his Excellency's letter. Upon reading it, Fr. Kondor's reaction was only increased disbelief. He sharply discredited the letter as a probable forgery, and offered to speak with the Bishop as soon as possible. He urged us to put our plans for leaving on hold. During those final months, Fr. Kondor never lost hope. And so, I myself encouraged Father Aloysius that all we needed was patience. The extreme reserve and prudence of the Bishop led all of us to believe that Fr. Kondor's interventions, if not already successful, would eventually clarify matters in our favor. Unfortunately, Fr. Kondor's good will never produced a change of mind in the Bishop and our departure from Fatima was delayed by over three months.

This delay in leaving Fatima had detrimental effects, not only in further deteriorating Father's health, but in creating the impression, as ugly as it was false, of wavering obedience on the part of Father Aloysius to the clear, written dispositions of his religious superiors. Where was the prompt obedience expected of any compliant religious subject?

When we most needed efficacious communication, mail from Rome was unbelievably slow on account of a prolonged postal strike in Italy. And telephone calls? Our phone calls appeared insufficient to depict our actual situation in Fatima, perhaps because we were obliged to use languages for which neither of the parties were native speakers.

Eventually another letter arrived from Father General, confirming the genuineness of the Bishop's first letter. A copy of the Bishop's second letter was enclosed. We had to pack up and leave. To lighten our work, Father Joaquin Maria Alonso, CMF,[3] who resided in Fatima, was assigned by the Superior General to help us attend to economic matters: the fate of the house of the Holm Oak and our small reserves in the local bank. We spent the last month selling all our furnishings and kitchen utensils. One by one, each of our

[3] Father Joaquin Maria Alonso, CMF, was among the experts at Vatican II, who helped work out the Trinitarian doctrine contained in *Lumen Gentium*. He also was a great mariologist and specialist on the apparitions of Fatima. He left behind an unfinished manuscript of several volumes on Fatima. He died suddenly in Madrid on the Feast of our Lady of Guadalupe, 1981.

members left Fatima, either to enter another seminary in the U.S. or, conquered by discouragement, to return to life in the world. Two seminarians, Jean Miville-Deschênes and I, decided to remain in Europe to continue our priestly formation. Father Alonso suggested we apply to the Major Seminary in Burgos, where Father Aloysius's ordination had taken place in 1929. We were accepted for the fall semester.[4] Among the many items in the house were the files. Father Aloysius told me to destroy all of them. I thought to myself, *This is something he himself may regret someday, and perhaps fairly soon.*[5] So, I waited, and

---

[4] Why, of all seminaries, did we go to Burgos? At the time of disbanding, Fr. Joaquin Alonso, CMF, was placed in charge of the two remaining seminarians in Portugal who wanted further studies; after the "exodus" of others who had freely decided for themselves other places to go, some eventually going to Brother Gino's in Italy. Father Alonso suggested we study either in Écône, Switzerland, or in Burgos, Spain, because both seminaries were "faithful to tradition." Luckily the other seminarian (Jean Miville-Deschênes) did not want to go to Switzerland, because he "already knew French" (being from Montréal), and so he preferred to learn Spanish. I agreed with him, and because of that simple decision, we were saved from imminent danger, because the Swiss seminary was eventually excluded from the Church because of its ultra-traditionalist beliefs, under the leadership of Archbishop Lefebvre. I am grateful for the solid education I got in Burgos. The Archdiocesan Seminary had changed somewhat in the period after Vatican II, but without going too far. Undergraduate studies are never the time to experiment in new ideas.

[5] The only document I destroyed was the first letter from the Bishop of Leiria Fatima, dated March 1, 1973, refusing to approve us on account of "[Father's] age and his state of health." At the end of the letter, he

eventually helped Father to realize we would need these documents. Regarding these files, as well as many other matters, I could not bear to see Father in a state of such sadness. My only recourse was to continue telling him, "God is great. He can raise us up somewhere else in the world." Inside myself, I was far from feeling convinced we had any future. I simply could not find better words to pour something like a diluted balm over his wounded spirit. He who had healed so many others, who had so often healed my own soul, did he not deserve some small reward in return?

Finally, on August 1, 1973, I accompanied Father Aloysius on a flight from Lisbon to Los Angeles. When he heard the engines revving up, he immediately surfaced out of that deep well in which during the past several months he had struggled futilely to find light. He remained awake, saying rosaries the entire trip. When we arrived in Los Angeles, his first desire was to present himself to his Superior. This event held the greatest importance for him. Immediately after kneeling in front of his Superior, he poured out his soul to him. The following day, Father mentioned to me how totally relieved he felt, explaining, "From the depths of my humility, I went to confession."

---

adds: "It is painful for me to take this decision." I considered it also too painful to leave this letter around. Several years later I recuperated the letter by writing to the archivist of the Claretian Generalate in Rome. No longer is it discouraging. It is a proof text of what one of Father's confrères in the General Government once wrote to him: "Do not worry. If the work is from God no human power can stop it."

What need did you have? I thought, deeply impressed by his sensitivity and his prompt impulse to self-abasement. I had observed this attitude on other occasions in which he believed it necessary to recover what he supposed to be lost favor with God. I learned from this that what most authenticates a man's life is his willingness to admit the possibility of being mistaken.

Because the Sisters had initial approval, they did not make plans to leave Fatima. But their story had a sad ending. In the absence of their founder, they eventually could not go on in Fatima. After seeking advice in Rome, they wandered about in search of a place to put down their roots. Understandably, the storm had been too great for their little boat. They soon disbanded and to date have never reconstituted.

After leaving Father in Los Angeles, I went to Spain on August 22, 1973. During the next five years, at the Archdiocesan Seminary of Burgos, I completed my philosophy and theology studies. I kept in continual contact with Father Aloysius. Some of his letters, most of which deal directly with the foundation of the Missionaries of Perpetual Adoration, are included in the Appendices. The fact the Order survived proves the power of God alone, but the value of Basque tenacity is not to be underestimated.

About a year and a half before I completed my studies, Fr. Richard Konen spoke to his newfound Bishop (D. Miguel Gonzalez Ibarra, of Ciudad Obregon, Sonora) about Father Aloysius's disbanded project. In February 1977, the Bishop went to visit Father Aloysius in Los

Angeles, and agreed to accept our community in his Diocese. The Bishop designated Alamos, a small colonial town on the western slopes of the Sierra Madre, an ideal place for us to reconstitute. He even provided a large old motel and grounds, at a most modest price, for our beginnings. Our budding community arrived in mid-June, 1977. Five young men had been selected among those who had become enthusiastic about the project after Father's return to Los Angeles. I was not able to accompany them at first, as spring semester in Burgos was not over until the end of June. The day the five new members first arrived by bus, they walked to the "monastery," and were told by a resident of Alamos that the town was suffering a severe, protracted drought, and to "pray for rain." They took this petition to heart. Through the front gates of the monastery they walked up the driveway and knelt down in the patio to pray for rain. Rain drops started falling immediately!

On September 2, 1977, our Congregation was given its initial recognition by the Bishop as an Association of the Faithful. The ceremony began at the parish church of Alamos, with the Bishop performing the following: (1) he ordained me to the diaconate; (2) he led the procession with the Blessed Sacrament in a monstrance held above his head to the motel (transformed into a monastery) where he installed the Most Blessed Sacrament in our chapel (provisionally the third-floor lookout room); (3) he then issued a decree which outlined his will that our Congregation of Missionaries of Perpetual Adoration be a new foundation in his Diocese of Ciudad Obregón. The decree is in our annals and is signed by all the persons who participated in the event.

Our Order continued in full contact with Father Aloysius, by letter and by phone, until his death in 1981 of congestive heart failure, complicated other heart problems. He also had hip replacement operations. Although in general Father never lost his mental clarity, in the last year or two of his life congestive heart failure may account for certain limitations to his accustomed sharpness. He was helped by Kevin Manion who served him as a full-time caregiver.[6]

One incident, told by his personal secretary, Fr. Kevin Manion, to our community in Alamos, deserves repeating. When Father Aloysius left his monastery for the last time to be taken to the hospital where he was to die, he already knew he would never return. For three minutes he stood deathly still in his tracks. Speechless, and with his eyes conveying an all-consuming fear, Father was asked what was the matter. With a solemn and faltering voice, barely audible, he replied: "And what if... I... am condemned!" Father Kevin immediately encouraged him— "But Father, you always taught us as our motto the words of Holy Scripture: 'Let us go with confidence to the throne of grace, and we will find mercy'" (*Heb.* 4:16). Father then

---

[6] Fr. Kevin Manion was ordained in 1989 at the Basilica of Our Lady of Zapopan in Guadalajara as a diocesan priest. In 2014 he initiated the cause of beatification of Father Aloysius, which continues under the auspices of the Archdiocese of Los Angeles.

lifted himself with determination and walked feebly toward the car that would take him to the place of his calvary.

On April 6, 1981, after several days of excruciating pain, Father died in a secular hospital, a man completely unknown to—but evidently venerated by—the personnel who attended him.[7] Father Kevin Manion, the sole eye-witness, narrated to our community the gruesome details, for example, Father's sharp reactions to the "code blues" that he was periodically administered. Father Manion showed us some of the bloodstained clothes as well as the tubes that were inserted into his respiratory and digestive tracts. This death shared in the "scandalous" aspects of Christ's own death which, as St. Mark described it, all but destroyed the Faith of his first disciples. This was real, unadulterated *dereliction*, and we were shivering at the details narrated to us. Later on, when I searched for the possible significance of April 6, I was surprised to discover the original Last Supper had fallen on that date. Since Holy Thursday was Father's greatest inspiration in life, no day appears to be more significant for his death.

On two or three occasions Father had prompted me: "When I die, are you coming to my funeral?" He expected me to reply in the negative. Why? The reason for this and for several other dispositions toward me and other members of the order was his firm insistence that we were not to draw attention to the new foundation. To draw attention created "confusion." Confusion led to high blood pressure. High

---

[7] Western Park Hospital, Los Angeles.

blood pressure led to heart attack... But could that matter any longer after his death? To him, apparently it would. He had coaxed this promise from me, so I did not attend the funeral.[8] In any case, death itself would not separate him from our work. As Bishop Arzube recalled in the funeral homily, Father Aloysius had once said: "I will do much more from Heaven than I could do on earth."

SINCE FATHER'S DEATH, his grave at San Gabriel Mission always bears flowers from simple persons who come to ask his intercession. I have heard a few testimonies from persons who have received favors after his death. On one occasion, a married woman from Alamos, who was declared sterile by her doctor, told me she was going to Los Angeles. So I suggested she visit Father's grave to ask for the gift of fertility. Five years later she returned to Alamos to tell me she had given birth to three children.[9]

Over the past thirty-eight years, many people have asked about Father Aloysius's cause for Beatification and Canonization. "Father Aloysius, I firmly believe, will be canonized one day," says the author Patricia Treece.[10] In 1996, Jeff Moynihan wrote to then Cardinal Roger Mahony

---

[8] A 38-year afterthought: I might have followed Fr. Aloysius's other advice—to ask the Guardian Angels to make me invisible.

[9] In my first edition, I mistakenly stated she had visited Father's grave. After publishing, she rectified this error of mine, but she strongly affirmed that this miracle was through Father Aloysius's intercession.

[10] Patricia Treece, *Messengers: After Death Appearances of Saints and Mystics* (Huntington, Indiana: Our Sunday Visitor, 1995), p. 188.

of Los Angeles on this matter. The Cardinal's written reply is in our files. I quote the main body of his letter:

> Any cause for declaration of a holy life or sainthood is begun by the group which has the canonical responsibility. In the case of Father Aloysius Ellacuria, CMF, the Claretian Community is the appropriate body to institute any such proceedings.
>
> You might wish to pursue this more with the Claretians to see whether or not they might discern this as a possible cause for a holy life and worthy of consideration by the Congregation [for the Cause of Saints].
>
> Please keep in mind that well over 99% of holy people in the life of the Church are never formally beatified or canonized.[11] Rather, they live out their holy lives as wonderful signs of their commitment to Christ, and their sanctity is recognized at the local level.
>
> Please also keep in mind that any of these processes involves many years—usually decades—of extraordinary work and very high expense. Because of these factors, it is quite rare to institute these processes with the Congregation [for the Cause of Saints].[12]

---

[11] Charles Péguy states the same idea thus: "It is obvious that there are infinitely more obscure saints than public saints... Now we recognize as one of the stoutest propositions of our faith that God makes no difference between the ones and the others, and that they receive the same crowns" *Basic Verities* (Chicago: Regnery, 1965), p. 113.

[12] Letter dated September 5, 1996, and quoted with permission of Cardinal Roger Mahony. In an earlier letter to Jeff Moynihan, the Cardinal states (among other things): "While I did not know Father Aloysius personally, nonetheless I have heard of the wonderful ways in which he extended himself in pastoral ministry to countless thousands of people throughout Southern California" (July 26, 1996). The general attitude among the Claretians appeared favorable to introducing Father Aloysius's cause for sainthood.

One of the more significant proofs of Father's "doing more from Heaven" is the survival of his little Order which, in spite of innumerable difficulties and limitations, continues marching forward with hope in our hearts.

SINCE THE FIRST EDITION of this book eighteen years have passed. Thus I wish to include here significant facts about the process for the Beatification of Father Aloysius.

About ten years ago Fr. John Raab, CMF, announced after the Memorial Mass of Father Aloysius in San Gabriel Mission that the Claretians were unable to start the process for the Beatification of Father Aloysius because the Claretians were in overload with numerous martyred members of their Congregation from the Spanish Civil War (1936-39). Soon after this announcement, Fr. Kevin Pius Manion made the decision to initiate the Cause by submitting a petition for sainthood, in March, 2011, to the Archbishop of Los Angeles, His Excellency José Gómez. With the Archbishop's Decree of September 8, 2014, the Private Association of the Christian Faithful was established, according to Canon 299, §3, for the "Beatification and Canonization of Father Aloysius Ellacuria, CMF." Updates on the Cause are provided by the Claretian Missionaries of the USA-Canada Province.

On April 6, 2013, I was asked to preach the homily at the Memorial Mass for the Servant of God, Father Aloysius at San Gabriel Mission. Since the Church emphasizes the virtues more than miracles in candidates for sainthood, I chose seven of the virtues I believe Fr. Aloysius practiced to a heroic degree. This homily is included at the end of the book (Appendix F).

The road to beatification has changed a great deal in our times. Formerly, the Church did not allow a Cause to be introduced before fifty years had elapsed from the time of the candidate's death. The reason: to avoid being influenced by excessive enthusiasm surrounding a holy person's life; that is, to see things more objectively. There is much to be said for this position. Today, however, the Church prefers the Cause to be introduced at least before thirty years have elapsed. The reason: to take depositions from the witnesses while a sufficient number of them are still alive. This also makes much sense.

Nonetheless, in the more recent past, we have seen the Church take a new attitude, on account of the sheer number of recently deceased persons who are being presented for sainthood. In some sense, it has become "popular" to be canonized, as if it were a trophy we feel obliged to reward our best and holiest friends. We all know we cannot canonize anyone while they are still alive. But, once they are buried, many would like to put their candidate on fast track, and if it were possible, by popular acclaim. We all remember Vatican Square packed with shouting fans immediately after Pope John Paul II's death: "Santo Subito! Santo Subito!" On March 10, 2016, the Vatican announced new financial regulations about beatification, because it has become so expensive: 500,000 Euros on an average. Some people have gone overboard, thinking that everything depends on material human efforts. A poor man like San

Juan Diego took 450 years to be canonized. St. Joan of Arc, from the 15th Century, was finally canonized in 1922.

In November of 2016 the Bishops of the United States at their regular meeting, gave their "placet" in a unanimous vote in favor of the Cause of Father Aloysius. A year later, on November 17, 2017, the Archdiocesan Commission for the Canonical Inquiry was formally established at the Chancery Office of Los Angeles. At this stage, our Founder can now be called the Venerable Servant of God.

The Cause of Father Aloysius is most blessed to have one of the greatest experts entrusted with such causes, Dr. Andrea Ambrosi, who resides in Rome. He has successfully done many important sainthood causes. Even with such an expert it is not a short process and we must exercise patience, willing to accept, above personal preferences, the Holy Will of God. In the end, echoing what a priest confrere of Fr. Aloysius said about his work for our Order: "What God wants, no human power can stop."

The Claretians are in the process of opening a special office to help those visitors and devotees of Father Aloysius for the pilgrims who visit his grave at San Gabriel Mission. For those interested, please contact the Mission at (626) 457-3035.

VIII.

The Alamos Monastery and the Mission in the Yaqui Valley

WHAT HAPPENED IN SONORA

Up to this point, the final chapters of the biography of Father Aloysius Ellacuria, C.M.F., have dealt with his years in Fatima, Portugal, founding our religious Congregation (1971–73); the uprooting from Fatima (August 1, 1973); and our replanting in Alamos, Sonora, Mexico, four years later.[1] During the last eight years of his life,—he died on April 6, 1981—Fr. Aloysius maintained contact with us by letter and telephone; and we occasionally visited him in Los Angeles, with our guardian angels making us invisible, of course. This final chapter deals with what happened after Father Aloysius's death. The hope of reestablishing ourselves somewhere else, although it seemed unrealistic to all of us, including to Father Aloysius, never completely vanished during the four years following Fatima. The initial move to Mexico is treated briefly at the end of our last chapter. We must now spell it out in more detail.

In Los Angeles, Fr. Aloysius, as was his custom, continued receiving several young men for spiritual counseling, some of whom wished to live by the ideals he had taught in Fatima. He sent five of them for initial seminary training to Holy Apostles' Seminary in Cromwell,

---

[1] *The Life of Father Aloysius*, 2001, pp. 79–107.

Connecticut.[2] Eventually a Bishop in Sonora, Mexico, learned about us in 1976, through the intervention of Fr. Richard Konen.

Alamos is a historic town where Coronado camped in 1531 on his way north, to find the Seven Cities of Gold, as legend tells. The parish church of the Purísima Concepción has baptismal certificates dating from 1682, although earlier unrecorded missionary activity must have taken place there, particularly with the Jesuits: Father Pedro Mendez (†1643), and Father Eusebio Kino (†1711), and others.

Our first great difficulty in adapting to this small colonial city was the intense heat from May to October, coupled with scarcity of drinking water. Some of the bedrooms had 1950's grocery-store ceiling fans imported from the United States. Our water came from a deep but dangerously contaminated well, as it was situated near a populated area, in a low vacant lot near the dry Aduana Creek out front. This creek is dry most of the year except during flash floods in the ten-week monsoon season. Since 1977, we have had three droughts, each lasting anywhere from eight to ten years. Our house was an abandoned motel which never flourished during its ten years of operation (1959–68). On closing in 1968, it was purchased by Alfonso Robinson Bours, who immediately donated it to Bishop Miguel Gonzalez Ibarra, who ten years later in 1977 sold it to our Board of Directors, a group of seven laymen appointed by Fr. Aloysius who met with him in Los Angeles in the final years of his life, and continued meeting afterwards without him. Between 1968 and 1977, the Diocese of Ciudad Obregón used this motel for weekend

---

[2] This is a seminary for adult vocations. Our "MAP" seminarians did their further ecclesiastical studies later on in Guadalajara, Mexico.

retreats held by Catholic lay groups, and generally for other religious purposes. The day we arrived we actually found a troupe of screen actors departing from the motel after having worked several months on the movie "México Norte."[3] Alamos has long been a center for artistic activity: music festivals, talent contests, and art shows. It becomes extremely crowded and noisy on weekends, especially at night, because the curfew is at 2:30 a.m., and no one respects it. (The parties out front in the creek area seem to be just beginning at 10:30 p.m. and end around 5:30 a.m.) The architectural layout often inspires visitors to take out their easels and sit in the main plaza attempting to capture on canvas something of the Spanish colonial period to take home with them, or to present at the next art show.

Very little had to be done to make over the old "Motel Alamos" for our purposes. In basic structure it had the bare essentials for a monastery. A lot of hard work on important details was needed. In a few years it actually reached the semblance of a monastery. Since the original owner of the house was a man surnamed Macías, someone suggested it had now turned into the "House of *Messias*."[4] If Don Quixote envisioned wayside inns as castles, we too needed some of that quixotic gift to see this 24-room white elephant as a monastery. An extra-large dose of spiritual imagination from the Holy Spirit could transform this old building into a home for Fr. Aloysius's new foundation. Father's actual expression was that our monastery should be a "showcase."

---

[3] A western movie, directed by Emilio Fernández, using the picturesque hills and streams around Alamos for cowboy skirmishes. The 200-year-old Alamos parish church was used for a wedding scene, with the then Associate Pastor, Fr. Felipe González Iñiguez, featuring in the role of the priest, and Silverio Valenzuela, the then sacristan, as acolyte.

[4] Anselmo Macías was a Mexican Army General and the Governor of Sonora from 1939–43.

We're fortunate he never came down here to see the reality. Over the years we have continued, with elbow grease, to make over what God had so generously provided, actually spoiling us, complete with a bathroom in each room. The motel restaurant became the dining room; the cantina, the library (so, we're 'bookaholics'); two rooms in a separate building were joined to make a chapel. Only two additions were made: the basketball court in the orchard and a stone fountain in the patio. Contrasted with the huts made of branches which the first Franciscans and other primitive communities had to start with, we were living in a five-star hotel. If God was spoiling us, He would eventually provide enough crosses for the work to deserve being His own.

When we arrived in 1977, vocations were regular in coming. Young men rang the bell at the front gate, harboring varying degrees of certainty about God's will for them. Some would decide to stay more than a week, and it was always easy to house ten or twelve young men. The ongoing turnover replaced those who left at different stages of formation. This was normal in most religious communities in the northwest of Mexico. The central highlands of Mexico, however, were famous for having numerous vocations. That was "martyr country" in the late 1920s. When Pope St. John Paul II visited the Major Seminary in Guadalajara in 1979, there were approximately 600 major seminarians, and another 600 minor seminarians in that Archdiocese alone. Things have changed in the last 40 years, not only in Mexico, but everywhere. The trend spirals ever downward. In our Fatima period, Fr. Richard Konen told us something astounding.[5] He had first entered the Jesuits in 1951. In that

---

5 Fr. Richard Konen, born April 19, 1933, in Jersey City, NJ, was a co-founder for his role in getting us into the Diocese of Ciudad Obregón, Sonora. As mentioned in my first biography of Fr. Aloysius, he died at age 80, on December 20, 2013, in Lourdes Hospital, Navojoa, Sonora.

year, 300 candidates showed up for the novitiate, in the New York Province alone! They had to be divided into three groups—100 for each novitiate class. In Alamos we learned quickly not to suffer too much from seeing fewer new faces, nor from the invariable separation anxiety when candidates decided to leave. Today we are consoled by God's generosity in sending us two or three each year, and we are convinced that those who are truly called persevere. Some years ago, a priest in charge of formation at the Diocesan Seminary in Obregón City said our work as educators is like that of Sisyphus, in Greek mythology, whose eternal fate was to push a heavy stone up to the peak of a high mountain. Following the analogy, a formator may exert himself several years encouraging seminarians. Then, when the top is almost in sight, his promising disciple slips and rolls back to the bottom! In general, less than ten percent persevere to ordination, and I think it has always been that way. This should sadden no one. It has never been easy to select candidates. And, in any event, God often uses seminarians and novices for outstanding futures in the life of the Church and the world.[6] For those who persevere, however, under adverse circumstances, great fortitude is given by God to depend on Divine Providence. We are made to discover, usually in hindsight, how the negative factors serve to *favor* true sanctity more than all human advantages. (Again, look at the lives of the Saints.)

None of us were priests in the summer of 1977. So Fr. Aloysius appointed Martin Brenner, a new convert from Judaism to Catholicism, to be our first local Superior, as he was the eldest among us. His conversion story would make

---

[6] For example, Blessed Anacleto González Flores, martyr (†1927), and many others, whether famous or unknown.

an amazing chapter in itself.[7] He was a good and dedicated Superior who learned Spanish in only two months. In the extreme summer heat, he took us every afternoon to Cuchujaqui, a creek in the woods eight miles away, where we submerged ourselves in the cool mountain water. He daily taught us solid Catholic doctrine, and after evening meal provided a wholesome environment for community life with conversations and table games. Then we would end our day with Holy Hour at 8:00 p.m., Compline, and Grand Silence until 8:00 next morning. We went daily to the Parish Church for 6:00 a.m. Mass.[8]

The Pastor at the parish church was Fr. Joseph Brackett, originally from Pennsylvania. His assistant was Fr. Felipe González Iñiguez, a priest from Yahualica, Jalisco, who, like everyone from the highlands of Jalisco, are thoroughly saturated in their faith; many of them have relatives martyred in the Cristero War (1926–29). Fr. Brackett was 52 years of age when we arrived. He was a true missionary who had already been working in different parts of Sonora for twenty years. He spent most of his days traveling in a small pickup or on a burro through the innumerable outlying villages, celebrating Masses.[9] Our

---

[7] While a student at UCLA, he signed up for a course on the History of the Catholic Church. He arrived the first day late to class. The professor was explaining the origin of the Church at Pentecost, reading Acts 2, on the Descent of the Holy Spirit. At that moment Martin experienced the powerful infusion of the Holy Spirit into his own soul, totally changing his life's direction.

[8] Martin Brenner left our community approximately a year later, before taking vows. After studying theology on his own at the Angelicum in Rome, he eventually married and had nine children. He taught theology at American seminaries, and died in Bloomfield, Michigan, on June 29, 2016.

[9] Msgr. Ismael Esparza, a former Pastor of Alamos, counted 300 small rural communities in this Parish.

Founder placed him in charge, as a more-or-less distant overseer. When we, in this strange environment, saw our insignificance and felt so unsure of ourselves before such huge numbers of unchurched people, he said, "we could do more here than anywhere in the United States, *by our presence alone.*"[10] It was Fr. Brackett who urged a fervent young parishioner, Ismael Figueroa, to knock on our door.

Ismael Figueroa-Carrasco, a member of the extended Figueroa family of Las Cabras and Alamos, joined us a few months after we arrived.[11] He is one of the quietest persons you ever will meet, but a great narrator when it is time to preach. He spent many years meditating the Holy Scriptures and memorizing the Letters of St. Paul word-for-word. To this day, as a priest, he is totally dedicated to the missionary life, similar to Fr. Brackett, his first mentor. The younger, more recent missionary priests in our congregation are presented in color, and with a biographical sketch, on our website.[12]

Among key persons in the parish Church of Alamos at that time, I can point out Balvanera ("Nelita") Bours, who died on September 1, 2011. Both she and her aunt, Madre Carmelita Bours, a nun in the order of the Missionary Daughters of the Most Pure Conception, were persons who simply radiated sanctity.[13] Nelita was a member of a secular institute, founded by a Claretian priest, Fr. Luis Núñez, C.M.F. These women and several other lay persons in

---

[10] After twenty more years of missionary labor in Sonora, Fr. Brackett eventually returned to the United States, to his Diocese of Gallup, New Mexico, and died in Albuquerque on October 31, 1999.

[11] Some of the Figueroa ancestors are said to have migrated to Los Angeles on the De Anza Trail in 1775, and gave their name to Figueroa Street, which runs parallel to the 110 or "Harbor" Freeway.

[12] www.missionariesoffatima.org

[13] Madre Carmelita's body later was found incorrupt.

Alamos, whose names could fill several pages, provided a chorus of inspiration for us. No one is more fervent than a Mexican who truly believes in his religion, and most of them do. I knew an American priest who, when he was in Rome as a seminarian, decided to move to Mexico because he could here, "fully drink in the faith." When I lived in Guadalajara for four years, I liked to go to the Church of St. Nicholas of Bari on Mondays, because they hold a novena to this Saint, and it takes up several Masses every Monday. Just watching the faithful, both young and old, coming into this church to express their heartfelt devotion, could convert a hardened sinner in an afternoon.

A devout person in Alamos once mentioned to me that we should learn to be more affable on the streets. Although I was taken aback by this remark, I examined my conscience and the conduct of myself and our community in general. I realized we were taking things so seriously, that our facial expressions were enough to put people off. In part, it had to do with our Father Founder's wish that we never clown around or crack jokes in the community, as he believed that would make us "chirping birds," with no spiritual substance in us. This is true, especially when jokes become corny or ridicule holy things. Although it was true that Father Aloysius wanted us always to have a gentle smile on our faces, we tended to ignore this part of his teaching, because we were novices and dead serious about our new way of life, all the while unsure about what it really meant. Our attitude became more conspicuous from the fact that now we were living in a town of only 5,000 souls. All of us, except Ismael, were from a large metropolis, concretely from Los Angeles and San Diego, where people rarely greet each other on the streets. (Today, whenever I arrive from Alamos to Los Angeles, I make the mistake of greeting people on the streets, at least the first day, and people think I'm nuts.) But, what about the grave demeanor of Father Aloysius himself, which no one who knew him will deny. He never laughed out loud, nor can he be classified as a person with a sense of humor. He did not wish us to act light-heartedly. A few years ago, I came across a statement in a book by Thornton Wilder:

> A sense of humor judges one's actions and the actions of others from a wider reference and a longer view and finds them incongruous. It dampens enthusiasm [. . .] It recommends moderation. This wider reference and longer view are not the gifts of any extraordinary wisdom."[14]

This observation of Thornton Wilder helped me to better understand the attitude of our Father Founder about acting seriously as missionaries. There was a purpose behind it. At the same time, we learned to adapt to an environment that was so different from our origins.[15] Mexicans are very affectionate. They greet and take leave of each other with what outsiders often consider overdone emotion. But here it is completely sincere interchange. In any case, since our spirituality is Ignatian-Teresian, a good mixture of St. Teresa's teaching on this matter can help us. She says we need to be as friendly as possible to those around us.[16]

---

[14] *The Eighth Day* (Harper and Row, New York, 1967), p. 209.

[15] The culture of Mexico is considered by one author to be entirely different from its neighbor's to the north. Alan Riding, in his book *Distant Neighbors*, says that no two countries are closer to one another geographically, and further apart culturally, than Mexico and the United States. If Mexicans were punctual, it would be one of the richest countries on earth. But, their leisurely attitude contributes to a contemplative environment which is a great advantage for a budding religious congregation.

[16] "Try then, sisters, to be as pleasant as you can, without offending God, and to get on as well as you can with those you have to deal with, so that

MY FIRST CONTACT WITH ALAMOS was on July 17, 1977. Arriving by bus from Tijuana in 18 hours, I was overwhelmed by the hot Sonora desert. Previous to Alamos I had lived four years in the diocesan Seminary of Burgos, Spain, which is the second coldest place in Spain after Soria.[17] After two weeks in Alamos, I went completely dehydrated, and was taken 32 miles to the Lourdes Hospital in Navojoa. I stayed there the entire month of August, because my blood pressure was too low: 90/70. One morning, the nurse, Sister Maria de la Salud Trujillo, came into my room at 7:00 a.m. and said, "Imagine! It was so hot last night that all the birds woke up dead [*Todos los pájaros amanecieron muertos*]!" During that month, two other members of our community had to be interned in the same hospital for the same reason. At the end of the month, the diocesan Bishop, Miguel González Ibarra, walked into my room and announced, "Get up, Carlos, because I am going to ordain you to the Diaconate on September 2nd." In a couple of days, I had to return to Alamos, and was ordained in the parish Church on schedule. The Bishop used the opportunity to draw up an edict for the establishment of our religious institute in his Diocese, and to officially install the Blessed Sacrament in our monastery. Many of our friends were present to sign the official document.[18] On September 13th, Fr. Aloysius called me to

---

they may like talking to you and want to follow your way of life and conversation, and not be frightened and put off by virtue. This is very important for nuns: the holier they are, the more sociable they should be with their sisters" (*The Way of Perfection*, ch. 41.)

[17] When St. Teresa was on the road to Burgos to found her last convent, Our Lord spoke to her, saying: "Do not let the cold of Burgos discourage you."

[18] In church law, our institute is a Public Association of the Faithful with the view of becoming eventually a full-fledged religious institute.

return to Burgos, Spain, to finish my theology requirements. I stopped in Los Angeles and visited with Father who gave me detailed instructions about what he wanted for our Constitutions and general plans for the house and grounds in Alamos.

Back in Burgos, regularly I received letters from Father Aloysius, as well as from the Alamos community of postulants and novices. Fr. Aloysius's letters are saved, and some have been published privately for members of our institute. I recall one letter from Alamos, in which the brothers described the hurricane "Elisa" which blew away one-third of our dining room roof in the fall of 1977. October is the month for hurricanes in the region, blowing in from the Pacific Ocean, bringing lots of rain.

After finishing my studies, I took the thirty-days Ignatian Spiritual Exercises along with 16 other priests, in Santander, a large coastal city on the Cantabrian Sea. Immediately after, I traveled southeast to Tolosa, in the Basque region, to stay one month with the community of Claretian priests, in order to type up the Constitutions of our Order, as they were being composed, chapter-by-chapter, by Fr. Timoteo de Urkiri, C.M.F., an expert both in Liturgy and in the constitutions of religious orders, according to the stipulations of Vatican Council II, and the desires of Father Aloysius. Fr. De Urkiri, when finished, said he had felt exceptionally inspired during the entire process adding, "The Holy Spirit works on the community in the Alamos monastery. So, these Constitutions have to be submitted to their actual religious life experience, and modified where necessary. As we say in Latin: *Primum vita, deinde lex.*"[19] Very little has been modified in them since then. We try to live our Constitutions as well as we can,

---

[19] "First life, then law."

knowing that our General Chapters can make modifications when deemed necessary, for example, when we decided to reduce the number of years from six to four, for the term of office of each Superior General.

On arriving back in Los Angeles in September, 1978, I spent many weeks with Father Aloysius, who fine-tuned his will about our Community in Alamos. He enthusiastically approved the Constitutions. Each day, for several hours, we would discuss important matters, specifically about living the religious spirit, with regularity in the observance of silence, cleanliness, and respecting cloistered areas in the house. And what seemed to hold tremendous importance for him was the orchard. He described in detail many different types of fruits and vegetables that he wanted us to cultivate, and that grow in tropical regions. This was difficult for us, because all of our members wanted to become priests, and studies occupied most of their time. In the early days, all manual labor was concentrated on maintaining the house and grounds in proper order. When it was a motel, the owners had employed about 20 workers just to keep it clean and operating. I am happy today that our youngest priest takes after our Father Founder since he has a green thumb. He takes our postulants and novices into the orchard every day and works with them. They are just fascinated with this work. When Fr. Heriberto asked me what our Founder would think of this, I replied that he will be overjoyed that finally something so positive is being done in the orchard.

In July of 1980, Fr. Aloysius sent us another vocation, Fernando Cesario Ferrer Ramírez, who was born in San Marcos, Texas, on February 25, 1933. Although he was already 47 years of age, he was well recommended by Fr. Aloysius because he had been Fr. Aloysius's novice some thirty years earlier. He left the seminary in the 1950's and worked 18 years as a probation officer in Los Angeles, California, in charge of several other probation officers. When his desire to become a priest welled up in him again, he visited Fr. Aloysius who told him about our community in Alamos. We started to call him by his second name "Cesario," because that is the name his mother first gave to him on the birth certificate, before adding "Fernando" on the baptismal certificate. He was received for perpetual vows in a short time because he was already well prepared for it by his original training under Fr. Aloysius. After completing ecclesiastical studies in the Major Seminary of Guadalajara, he was ordained to the priesthood on August 15, 1988, in the Cathedral of Ciudad Obregón. He was very hard working in the formation of our future missionaries, both in Guadalajara and in Alamos, as well as doing pastoral work in the parishes. He had very good health, being very athletic, as well as ascetic in eating habits. This is why he surprised us by dying suddenly, in the odor of sanctity, on July 3, 2015, from an acute appendicitis. He contributed very much to our community by his religious fervor and perfect observance of the rules as he had learned them from Father Aloysius.

In November of 1996, Bishop Vicente Garcia Bernal, invited (or begged) us to take on the Parish Mission of San José de Bácum, a very small, poor farming town in the middle of the grain fields of the Yaqui Valley. Obviously no other priest in the Diocese wanted to take this task, because the town was a good example of where people go at night only half an hour from Ciudad Obregon to get drunk and act up, thinking no one will ever find out. At first I told the Bishop we were in no position to accept this commitment, as we could barely cover all the pastoral work we had in Alamos. The Bishop showed a real sad face, so I told him I would bring it up with our younger members right away.

Three of our members were deacons scheduled to receive the priesthood in December, 1996. In spite of their youth, or better, because of it, they jumped at the opportunity. They told me it was most unfortunate I had disappointed the Bishop. So, I told them I would return immediately to the Bishop and tell him about their optimistic reaction. I thought to myself, *They don't know what they're getting into, and they'll be really sorry!* Their reaction was a terrific relief to the Bishop, and the following month Father Ismael Figueroa went to San José de Bácum to start the ball rolling. The deacons were busy with their ordinations in Alamos.

The church building in San José was large enough. However, there was no rectory, and so I transferred to that town and it took me a period of four years to get a four-bedroom rectory built, complete with chapel and other rooms to accommodate our religious community. As soon as the deacons were ordained (December 27, 1996) they came to help out, but because the rectory was not finished, we had to depend heavily on the people of the town in order to eat and sleep. The people, even those among them in dire poverty, were most generous to us. Besides San José itself, we have seven other small towns to attend to within the radius of that parish. Thank God our new priests were full of energy! They looked to me like young colts jumping for joy in their apostolate in the Yaqui Valley wheat fields.

Since 1996, as a Parish, San José de Bácum has changed almost beyond recognition. By the grace of God, the Rectory was finished, and five other buildings right in the same proximate area were built: parish offices, a 32-room retreat house, an old folks' home, a catechetical center, and now we are finishing the house of studies. Besides these buildings, we had to build four more churches for the outlying towns in our parish. After Almighty God, we owe most of this work to Father Elias Arambula, one of our most dynamic members. He also sings religious music to beautify the Valley, and far beyond.

We realized that to transform the Parish, the first item on the agenda was to evangelize the people. This is why we started giving retreats every weekend, and eventually building a retreat house to accommodate this pastoral work. People started coming from everywhere, even from other States in Mexico, to use this retreat house. If people are not evangelized, they cannot be expected to live like good Catholics. By starting with the spiritual, everything else fell into place. We did not need to look for money. God is generous with those who do His work with no other aim in sight.

Both Father Angel Enrique Olvera and I have taught for several years in the Diocesan Seminary of Ciudad Obregon which, fortunately, is situated near the town of Providencia, which is down the same road, and only 12 minutes from our Mission Parish.

We have not abandoned Alamos. However, with the incredible noise at night, especially on weekends, when parties right out front of the monastery use high-powered amplifiers, we wonder sometimes if God is not suggesting, not even subtly, that we look elsewhere to better train our postulants and novices. As Cardinal Robert Sarah writes in his now famous and prophetic book, *The Power of Silence: Against the Dictatorship of Noise* (2017), spiritual growth is impossible in a noisy world. Even if we remain in Alamos as a motherhouse, where we have the beautiful shrine of Our Lady of Fatima, we must think about formation first.

The main thing is to keep our eyes on Our Lady of Fatima. She takes such good care of us! And in Mexico, where the wonderful Mother appeared almost 500 years ago to San Juan Diego, we have found the perfect meeting between these two devotions. Every July we organize a

Pilgrimage to the Basilica of Our Lady of Guadalupe to take a few busloads of pilgrims from our Sonora desert almost a thousand miles to Tepeyac Hill to behold the miraculous tilma of St. Juan Diego. When Pope St. John Paul II prayed before this image, he affirmed to Her, "You live in this image." She, the same one who said to Juan Diego that he should not worry about anything, asked him, "Am I not here, I who am your Mother?"

Conclusion

In Fatima, if we learned anything from Father Aloysius, it was that the Blessed Mother makes herself present to us and to all people at any time and at any place in the world. All you need do is open your heart to Her constant maternal solicitations. The promise Father Aloysius made before he was miraculously healed—to spread the profound conviction of "Mary's loving, maternal presence to each soul,"—must surely be his foremost task in Heaven.

On July 13, 1917, Our Lady of Fatima declared: *Our Lord wishes to establish in the world devotion to my Immaculate Heart.* This is the message of Fatima in a nutshell, as well as our Father Founder's overriding aim in life. He realized that God Himself had chosen for our times this particular devotion as the most efficacious way to save souls. Father's life, then, may be summed up as an unceasing adoration of the Most Blessed Sacrament from his secure refuge in the Immaculate Heart of Mary. From her Heart, he would attract as many souls as possible to enter, like the Apostle St. John, into the Mother's new home of Ephesus. And he offered his new Congregation as a gift to that same most loving and Holy Heart to continue his work, through many "other St. Johns"—as he used to exhort his followers to become—by taking her into their own interior abode (cf. *Jn.* 19:27).

Father Aloysius was an extraordinary gift from God. In a postmodern world, he was that rare exception, who, to the secularist is shocking, to the consumerist scandalizing, but to those who receive the tiny flame of conversion, empowering. He is that living sign of contradiction that God raises up in difficult times to rally us to transcend ourselves so that we might live for God alone. He never believed this path was too hard for anyone. "There is only one thing that separates us from the Saints," he used to teach, "and it is faith." This faith, however, is not simply in the articles of the Creed, but in the practical consequences involved in living them out each day. Here we are on earth, surrounded by the heavenly hosts, with the Mother of God carrying us in her arms, and the Angels and Saints at our side. What does it mean to act at every moment according to these beliefs? Certainly social life involves many risks, the greatest of which is that of "losing one's self, to save oneself" (*Mk.* 8:35). With Father Aloysius's spiritual guidance and personal example, Christ's invitation to such a risk has become for countless souls an attractive adventure of love.

Many other things might have been said about Father Aloysius. Since he would have preferred that nothing be said about himself, considering himself as merely an unworthy instrument, it is my prayer that the reader may courageously continue the journey he pointed out toward the bright beacon of his life—to the Most Blessed Sacrament through the Immaculate Heart of Mary.

ANNOTATION TO CONCLUSION OF SECOND EDITION:

Father Aloysius in his later years, believed that the world was near its end. As he says in his letter of May 29, 1978, he bases himself, not only on what other great churchmen were saying, but on what he observed in the world around him, especially in reference to the corruption of society and the legalization of immoral practices, like abortion. Today, we see this has gone to even further extremes, with live-birth abortions, same-sex marriage, euthanasia, and drug addiction. And it seems it will get worse before it gets better. I myself, as I now have approached the age at which Father Aloysius left this world, feel the same as he did. How can things get worse when Our Lady of Fatima, over one hundred years ago, warned us of imminent danger? Since my first edition, it would seem we are at least in a great apostasy. Only Almighty God knows when the predicted "Great Apostasy" will come. This is why I use the indefinite article. But, because things are manifesting the departure of so many souls from the Church, I cannot pretend that everything is just fine, even if you, the reader, see me as a prophet of doom. Someone else has spoken much better than I can. So, I would like to give the final word to the littlest Saint in Heaven—St. Jacinta Marto who, in her last sickness in Lisbon, exclaimed: "Our Lady said that there are many wars and discords in the world. Wars are only punishments for the sins of the world. Our Lady cannot stay the arm of Her Beloved Son upon the world anymore. It is necessary to do penance. If the people amend themselves, Our Lord shall still come to the aid of the world. If they do not amend themselves, punishment shall come."

And yet, Our Blessed Mother promised: "In the end, my Immaculate Heart shall triumph."

Appendix A

The aims of the new Congregation of Missionaries of Fatima, written by our Founder, Father Aloysius Ellacuria, C.M.F., in October, 1972

Our full title is "Missionaries of Perpetual Adoration of the Most Blessed Sacrament and Perpetual Veneration of the Immaculate Heart of Mary." Our congregation is composed of priests, deacons, clerics, brothers, novices, postulants, and lay auxiliaries. Except for our lay auxiliaries, we live in community, and after the year of novitiate we profess simple vows of poverty, chastity, and obedience. We blend our contemplative and active life through prayer, penance, study and pastoral ministry. Jesus Christ has exhorted all of us through the holy Gospel to pray incessantly and take up our cross daily and deny ourselves thoroughly, and added to the Apostles: "Go into the entire world to preach the holy Gospel to every soul... in the name of the Father, the Son, and the Holy Spirit."

We firmly believe, for the success of our apostolic life, in the primacy and efficacy of prayer and penance. Without prayer and penance, there cannot be a fruitful active apostolate. The blending of prayer and penance unites us to God. In the measure of our union with God we are pleasing to Him. The more pleasing we are to God, the greater our influence with Him. The more influential we are with God, the greater our redemptive value with Christ, through Christ, and in Christ to save and sanctify immortal souls.

After being properly shielded with prayer and penance, our missionary congregation will be ready for the tasks entrusted to us, of spreading throughout the world a most ardent devotion to the Blessed Sacrament of the Altar and the Immaculate Heart of Mary, our Mother. It is around these two devotions that the entire message of Fatima revolves as is evident from the first apparitions of the Angel of Fatima in 1916, carrying the Holy Eucharist under both species, to the last dying words of Jacinta in 1920 in regard to our love for the Immaculate Heart of Mary, and to the pleadings of the Child Jesus to Sister Lucy in 1926: "What is being done to make known the devotion to the Immaculate Heart of My Mother in the world?"

We, Missionaries of Perpetual Adoration of the Most Blessed Sacrament and Perpetual Veneration of the Immaculate Heart of Mary, wish to imitate and preach the Immaculate Heart of our Blessed Mother in her love to the Holy Eucharist of her Divine Son, and likewise we wish to imitate and preach the love of Jesus to the Immaculate Heart of His most sweet Mother.

In our large communities, years to come, there should be perpetual adoration by day and by night. In our small communities, in our houses of studies, there must be at least three hours daily for our confrères before the Blessed Sacrament, two hours early in the morning, from six to eight, and another in the evening between eight and nine. Besides this adoration and veneration, respectively, of the Eucharistic Heart of Jesus and of the Immaculate Heart of Mary, imitating these two greatest gifts, our missionaries have other paramount intentions: first, perpetual reparation and atonement; second, perpetual thanksgiving; third, perpetual petition.

First, perpetual reparation to the Eucharistic Heart of Jesus and the Sorrowful Heart of Mary for all outrages, sacrileges and indifferences by which They are offended.

Second, thanksgiving: for all that we are and all that we have, through the infinite mercy of God.

Third, petition: praying that we live every day the Holy Thursday by increasing every moment a seraphic love towards

Jesus the Eternal High Priest, instituting the Holy Eucharist, the Holy Priesthood, and the New Commandment of Love. The life of the Missionaries of Perpetual Adoration should be a perennial reenactment of the mysteries of Holy Thursday.

Imitating Saint Anthony Mary Claret, we should pray constantly for the threefold grace: a) liberation of the Holy Souls from Purgatory; b) the perseverance of the just in sanctifying grace; c) the conversion of sinners; and we add, with Saint Camillus de Lellis, d) let us beg God to give us the charisma of assisting every person in their last agony, to obtain for them a happy and holy death. Concerning this last point, God will give this charism to the members of our congregation by their remaining faithful to grace. Our prayer for the dying should be ever abiding in us with the utmost compassion for them, in union with Our Lord on the Cross as he utters the word, "Sitio."

Our congregation that has begun in Fatima is so far the first congregation of men to have its origin on the holy grounds of the apparitions of our Blessed Mother in 1917 from May to October included. We Missionaries of Perpetual Adoration embrace wholeheartedly the mission to preach and practice the entire message that these wonderful apparitions in Fatima brought to the Catholic Church and to the whole world. We, dedicated by virtue of our vocation to the perpetual veneration of the Immaculate Heart of Mary, feel most privileged to preach and practice: a) a thoroughly filial and ever abiding consecration to the Immaculate Heart of Mary as her most devoted sons, exemplified by Saint John, the beloved Apostle, who received at the foot of the Cross, from the dying Christ, the Blessed Virgin as his own spiritual Mother and learned from her Immaculate Heart the manner and ways of her burning love for Jesus in the Most Holy Eucharist; 2) the Holy Rosary, in which we unite ourselves to Mary's Immaculate Heart in her intimate participation in the mysteries of Christ present sacramentally on our altars as our best Friend, our best Food, and our most consoling Viaticum in our last journey to a happy eternity; 3) the wearing of the holy scapular of Our Blessed Mother of Carmel, as the exterior sign of our interior consecration to the Immaculate Heart of Mary.

Our congregation hails as co-patrons: Saint Michael the Archangel, the glorious patriarch Saint Joseph, and Saint John the evangelist. Other patrons associated with our charism are: Saint Anthony Mary Claret, Saint Camillus de Lellis, St. Mary Michaela of the most Blessed Sacrament, and Saint Thérèse of the Infant Jesus.

Appendix B

Extract of letter from Father Aloysius
to then seminarian Charles Carpenter, Oct. 9, 1975

I am most positive about M.A.P.* I never have lived the
ideals of the M.A.P. so intensely, so fervently and so continuously.
Every Holy Mass up to the end of time, every sacramental tabernacle, are one with me to render our dearest Father in heaven
perfect adoration, thanksgiving, atonement and petition. It is
such an overwhelming happiness to approach our divine Father
through Christ, with Christ, and in Christ, the Eternal High Priest
and to enjoy the awareness of the adoption of sons telling him,
"Abba, Father." Abba in the Basque language means "spiritual
father" and that same word means Father of Fathers in Hebrew.

I have never enjoyed so much the recitation of the Our
Father and to be likewise one with Jesus and our two hearts
beating in unison for the glory of the Father, for the love of His
Mother, and his love to all Angels and Saints in Heaven and the
just on earth, and to live *in Corde Matris* (in the heart of the
Mother), and live her spiritual presence and travel all over the
world in her Immaculate Heart by visiting and assisting every
person at the hour of their death.

My dear Charles, I am, if I may say, divinely positive that
there is no higher ideal on earth than to live fully the threefold
ideals of the M.A.P. The Most Holy Eucharist, the Immaculate
Heart of Mary, and the salvation of all people in the supreme hour
of their death.

My sufferings have been very keen. Slanders have been
very unjust, and the one I felt most, when they slandered me to

---

* M.A.P. is the abbreviation for the official (Latin) name of the
Congregation: *Missioniarii Adorationis Perpetuae.*

Father *N*. The devil wanted, with that, to do away with the M.A.P. forever. I, so extra sensitive, found it very hard to sink into the very bottom of humility. The moment I did it, great peace came over me and also the sweetest, most tender love for Jesus and the Blessed Mother and souls, and perfect filial confidence in God, my Father. I feel now what Sister Mediatrix used to tell me in 1939–40–41–42, that she lived *in sinu Patris*, in the bosom of the Father. There are no words to express this properly; this is the way I feel, particularly in saying the Holy Mass.

During the day, I repeat constantly, "Praise, adoration, love and thanksgiving be every moment given to the Eucharistic Heart of Jesus in all the tabernacles of the world and to the end of time"... "Oh Sacrament most holy, Oh Sacrament divine, all praise and all thanksgiving be every moment Thine"... "Through Him, with Him, in Him, in the unity of the Holy Spirit, all glory and honor is Yours, Almighty Father, forever and ever. Amen."

I feel that my heart will continue rejoicing in my perfect peace and I am definite I will be able to give much more to souls now and from Heaven. I feel and see there is no hindrance or any curtain between God and my soul. Just the curtain of holy faith, which is very transparent.

My dear Charles, let us do our utmost to live fully our threefold aim. Let this be always and only our supreme endeavor on earth.

Your spiritual Father in the Most Blessed Sacrament and the Immaculate Heart of Mary,

[Signed] Father Aloysius Ellacuria, CMF

Appendix C

Words fail me now more than ever to express my deepest gratitude to Almighty God, through the Immaculate Heart of the Blessed Mother . . .

As I am nearing the end of my life, I am going to be seventy-three years old on the 21st of this coming June, it will be one of the greatest consolations of my supreme hour that I brought you all the way unto the Holy Priesthood. The other day, on the 24th of this month of May, your good Bishop Miguel Gonzalez Ibarra told me that he is going to make you another Christ, in the old Cathedral of Alamos. That was the cathedral, at one time, of all California and possibly other states also. It is a very historical place, and that cathedral will be given to your care so that you join the old with the new. You make all things new, in Christ, restoring all to Christ, *Restaurare omnia in Christo*. This was the motto of His Holiness Saint Pius X.

Your vocation is very great, my dearest spiritual son, your vocation is a gift of our God, the Almighty God, the good, good God, through the Blessed Mother and through your own parents and through your own uncles that were so violently and most painfully martyred, who are happily your intercessors in Heaven.

My dear Charley, do not ever get discouraged, never. The road ahead of you is going to be rather hard, the fruits of your labors are going to be scanty, apparently, and will be slow in coming into effect. Remember the Apostles, they had so many difficulties, and the Blessed Mother was always with them, so she will be with you...

I will be very near to you when I am in Heaven. You will not see me, but I will be very near to you, pleading constantly for your spiritual success, that Our Lord may sanctify you every moment through the mediation of the Immaculate Heart of the Blessed Mother...

While I feel that the progress of the new Congregation will be slow, you must rely on the Blessed Mother, who will help you to achieve the full message of our Lady of Fatima through this new Congregation, as her evangelists all over the world. At the same time this Congregation should be very solicitous and very compassionate with all the sick, all the poor, and all the destitute, particularly with all those who are near to death, by invoking the patronage of St. Camillus...

My dearest Charles, I don't know how long I am going to stay on earth. My mind is in eternity. I am constantly, uninterruptedly, united in spirit to every Holy Mass throughout the world, particularly at the consecration of each Holy Mass, offering every instant, perfect adoration, perfect thanksgiving, perfect atonement and perfect petition to the eternal Father, through Christ, with Christ, and in Christ the Eternal High Priest.

[Signed] Father Aloysius Ellacuria, CMF

Appendix D

Father Aloysius was unable to attend the vow ceremony of first members of MAP in Alamos on August 15, 1980. The following are extracts taken from the homily he wrote to be delivered in his absence.

Praise and thanksgiving be every moment given to the Most Holy and Most Divine Sacrament of the Holy Eucharist and blessed be the Immaculate Heart of our Blessed Mother.

Today, my dear sons, is your total consecration and total identification with Christ crucified. Total consecration means complete renunciation of anything sinful and worldly.

Today is your second baptism!

The Fathers of the Church assure us that religious profession is such an extraordinary act that it gives a plenary indulgence in regard to sin and temporal pain to the privileged soul that makes the religious profession. The Fathers of the Church also assure us that our Lord will not count, on the day of the Last Judgment, anything sinful or defective that the religious made before religious profession. Likewise, the Fathers of the Church assure us that people who have kept their religious profession will not be judged at the Last Judgment, but will sit gloriously with the Apostles to judge with Christ all the people.

Religious profession is a perfect holocaust, renouncing all the pleasures of sex, the riches of the world, and one's own judgment and will.

In my youth, I found my greatest joy not to take any sensual delight to give full pleasure to Christ and what is most costly to a young human being. I used to tell Christ, "I don't want any bit of this pleasure, to give you full pleasure. But by abstaining myself from this sexual act, I wish to be a father, a father of souls. And I want to save many, many souls by my abstaining myself from this sexual desire."

You, my dear *professandi,* do not have now many riches. You never know the plans of God upon you. People have given me money galore, thousands and thousands of dollars. I never felt the least attachment... My dear professandi, never be attached to money. The vow of poverty is to have a habitual, perfect detachment, even from the clothing or whatever one needs for oneself or for others.

The vow of obedience is to give up completely one's judgment and will and obey God, only God, always God in his superior and receive his utterances as words of God, even if the superior be imperfect, younger, even hostile to the religious. All this happens to people like myself, now seventy-five years old, who have had superiors whom I knew when they were in grade school, and I brought them to the congregation, and afterwards they became priests and superiors of my ailing age in life.

Because of this, my dear *professandi,* they call the vow of obedience well practiced a martyrdom; not so dolorous and painful and lasting a few hours, but the martyrdom of obedience well practiced lasts from profession until death.

I am now seventy-five years old. I made my first profession on the 15th of August, 1921. Our Lord, in His infinite goodness, has proven me with many sicknesses, seven major operations, six pneumonias, in danger of imminent death about six or seven times. I have been given the last sacraments several times. The other day I thought that my last day had come. My heart was so poor. I have many, many holy people, very many and very holy, who love me and who insist to God to keep me longer on earth. This past Saturday there were two holy Cubans before the Blessed Sacrament continually exposed in the Old Plaza Church, and I felt that after fifteen years of constant troubles of my heart, accentuated with almost unsurpassable

159

moral and physical afflictions... suddenly I felt relieved... so that I could rejoice with you now, my dear *professandi*, and I felt, after those fifteen years, that I have received a new heart. And so I am here with a new heart, with a baby heart, with a perfect heart to love you most tenderly and to love all souls most tenderly too, particularly the sick and the dying. Which, by the way, is one of the aims of the congregation of Perpetual Adoration of the Most Blessed Sacrament and Perpetual Veneration of the Immaculate Heart of Mary...

You, my dear sons, are called to be the Missionaries of Our Lady of Fatima par excellence. Yes, *par excellence*, continuing the work of Lucy, Francisco, and Jacinta. You, my dear sons, are called to a very high sanctity. St. Alphonsus de Liguori says that a religious, understood a good religious, is called to a very high sanctity and likewise a very high heaven.

My sons, God calls you to be heroes of sanctity, to go always upwards, swerving neither to the right nor to the left, always upwards as royal eagles. Never be afraid. Have the greatest joy. You must meet the Eucharistic Son. Do not be afraid. Your tenderest mother that will be your life, your sweetness and your hope, she will carry you most maternally, in her own Immaculate Heart. What an incomparable privilege and joy her own heart will have to take you right up to her first Son. What an incomparable privilege and joy to be ascending in the spiritual elevator of the Immaculate Heart while she is preparing you for the divine espousals with her divine Son; and finally with the mystical marriage or transforming union with the spouse of spouses, the Lover of lovers! Her God and your God! Her love and your love! Her and your own eternal bliss! Forevermore in the heavenly regions, distinguished among millions of the elect as the perpetual adorers of the Most Blessed Sacrament through the Immaculate Heart of the sweetest Mother of mothers.

Today, my dear sons, heaven is opened! All heaven is looking at this most famous cathedral of the New Vizcaya. This was the mother of the cathedrals of California, Arizona, and New Mexico. I am from the old Vizcaya. My language was uniquely Basque until I entered the seminary. Just see how the old Vizcaya and the new Vizcaya today are mystically united! So you are not only my brothers in Christ, but my blood brothers, and I love you, my dear Mexicans with all my being.

... This means, my dear sons, that the new congregation of the perpetual adorers of the Most Blessed Sacrament and perpetual venerators of the Immaculate Heart of Mary must increase fast in many nations and fly as royal eagles, as other St. John the Apostle, to save every soul with the special attraction for all the sick and the dying, and do all you can for them, and let your favorite ejaculation of the MAP be "Jesus, Mary, I love you, save all the sick and the dying the world over." And at the end of your lives, may the Dolorous and Immaculate Heart of Mary present all those souls at the foot of the dying Christ on Calvary and let His arms embrace and His Precious Blood give them, bestow on them, a kiss of pardon and peace, telling them as he told the good thief: "Today you shall be with me in paradise!"

Appendix E

Letter from Mrs. Susan Kaczmarczyk, April 6, 2000

Dearest Father Carpenter,

I am writing you about our son Matthew Louis Kaczmarczyk, and of the blessing from Father Aloysius Ellacuria.

Matthew was fourteen months old when he was diagnosed with Kawasaki disease. Every joint in his body swelled up, where he could not move at all any part of his body and before he could run and walk like all the rest of the little boys. Jerry and I took Matthew to Hurley Hospital where his doctor said to take him in Flint, Michigan. All the doctor could do for him was to give him forty baby aspirins a day and monitor this. The aspirins were for pain and swelling. His tiny fingers and toes were peeling, all the skin came off. Father, we could not see anything good from this, the doctors were getting ready to send Matthew to a children's hospital in Ann Arbor, Michigan for more test after test. In 1979, there was only one other case reported in the United States. That was the day we got a phone call at the hospital from Father Aloysius Ellacuria. And the blessing. I was at the hospital when they called me to come to the phone with Matthew. Father said to put the phone to Matt's chest and he prayed for a while, and within a few days Jerry and I took Matthew home cured of the disease.

It has been twenty years and we still have Father's picture and Matthew's picture near the Bible. Thanks to a very special and holy priest. We will always pray to him and also thank God for our many blessings.

This December Matt will graduate from Ferris State College, a blessed and healthy boy.

[Signed] Mrs. S. Kaczmarczyk

Appendix F

Homily delivered by Fr. Charles Carpenter, MAP,
at Mission San Gabriel on April 6, 2013

WHEN A CAUSE IS PROMOTED for beatification, the Church requires two miracles to prove that a person is in Heaven. But prior to that, the Church requires something even more important—the practice of virtue to a heroic degree.

Reflecting upon Father Aloysius Ellacuria, C.M.F., we see his life as a witness to many of the most important virtues. From my experience of having lived three and a half years in the same house with him, I recall seven virtues he practiced in an outstanding way: humility, fortitude, mortification, love, faith, magnanimity, and the virtue of religion.

1) <u>Humility</u>: Every night before retiring Claretian priests pray three Hail Marys for an increase of Humility, Purity, and Divine Love. I remember how Father Aloysius sat down on the steps of the Basilica at Fatima during Holy Week, 1973, because he considered himself unworthy to be a part of the ceremonies. This happened when he was suffering from congestive heart failure and our new religious community was going through the worst of trials. He accepted such humiliations with complete resignation.

2) <u>Fortitude</u>: It takes so much strength to withstand calumnies. This strength comes only from God. Father Aloysius said his greatest suffering came from calumny and slander. Although any priest who does his job well will experience some amount of calumny, such trials occur even more if the priest's reputation for sanctity extends beyond the customary degree. If he becomes famous, jealousy inspires hatred against him. St. Teresa of Avila said she suffered most when bad judgments and criticisms came to her from good persons.

163

3) <u>Mortification</u>: Father emphasized that the most important mortification to obtain purity is that of the eyes, "the floodgates of evil." How vital is this advice for our times, when governments no longer control pornography which has become rampant in the media and on the internet. Father used to tell us that the world, the flesh, and the devil are inviting us to "go ahead and take the pleasure offered by temptations to impurity." Father maintained his eyes shut about 80% of his waking hours. By rejecting temptations to impurity, he said we advance "millions of miles toward holiness."

4) <u>Love</u>: So consumed was he with the love of God, it was like sitting next to a huge furnace of God's love. He never stopped thinking about God. Deuteronomy commands us to "love God with all your heart, with all your soul, with all your strength" (*Dt.* 6:4). Father appeared to be doing this constantly. And fulfilling the second part of the Law, Father would visit the sick and the dying, and exhorted us to do the same. He really cared about other people, remembered each person's name, and never forgot to pray for them.

5) <u>Faith</u>: Father used to say that the only difference between the Saints and ourselves is their degree of Faith. This means that if we count on God more, God will do much, much more through each of us. This year I am teaching Philosophy of God and Epistemology in the Major Seminary. Both of these courses address the question of relativism, which Pope Emeritus Benedict XVI classified as the "dictatorship" of our times, and which Pope Francis continues to decry as the foremost error threatening our civilization.

6) <u>Magnanimity</u>: The term comes from Latin, meaning "greatness of soul". Paradoxically, this virtue dovetails perfectly with humility. A humble person is not a coward, but is brave in starting even great works for the glory of God. Fr. Aloysius was never afraid to be audacious in God's service. Josef Pieper, a great Thomist philosophy of the 20th century explains this virtue: "What indeed does magnanimity mean? Magnanimity is the expansion of the spirit toward great things; one who expects great things of himself and

makes himself worthy of it . . . Undaunted uprightness is the distinctive mark of magnanimity, while nothing is more alien to it than this: to be silent out of fear about what is true." [See Pieper's marvelous work: *The Four Cardinal Virtues*, Notre Dame University Press.]

7) <u>The Virtue of Religion</u>: After the three Theological Virtues, this is the most important virtue. It is classified under Justice, because it has to do with "giving what is due", in this case due honor, worship, and thanksgiving to God. This is the virtue I believe most stands out in Father Aloysius. From the time he was just a postulant (15 years old) he wore scapulars and medals, and because of his extreme devotion, was looked upon by his superiors as being perhaps "too" religious. So, he prayed to St. Rita of Cascia, known for resolving impossible cases, and she obtained for him the grace of being admitted into the Novitiate. During his entire life he manifested this vertical dimension of continual dialogue with God. This "continual dialogue" is the central idea in Benedict XVI's famous book *Jesus of Nazareth*, where our Pope Emeritus defines Jesus as a continual dialogue with God the Father, who invites us to join Jesus and live in the same manner. To see Fr. Aloysius was to witness his "continual dialogue" with God.

WHEN WE IMITATE HOLY PERSONS, we must not make the mistake of attempting to imitate their charisms, but rather their virtues. The Church raises holy persons to the altars for that very purpose, so that we may have good examples to imitate in following Christ as perfectly as possible.

Let us pray for the promotion of Father Aloysius to Beatification and Canonization. No one can "buy" this grace, so we do not ask for money for the cause, but for prayer. It is a sheer gift of God.

Acknowledgements

The present book owes its existence to several persons who, directly or indirectly, have helped me to begin, to continue, or to persevere until it was finished. An oversight in acknowledging anyone's assistance is certainly possible on account of the large number of persons along the road who rendered some service.

First of all, my religious community, who encouraged me to tell them about our Father Founder, generously provided the spiritual and material support, and bore up with my absences during this project.

To Jonathan Nguyen I am most grateful for providing me with a laptop, and his many hours of technical assistance in getting the second edition adapted to printing specifics; to Thérèse Buehner for printing out the rough drafts; to Fr. Alfred Hernandez for providing me with the time needed at his rectory to revise the entire work; to Philip Wood for delivering print-outs and other materials to me, to Emily Smiley and Russell Richer for proof reading the final text.

May Our Lord reward each of these persons, as well as countless others, who have contributed in some way to the eventual realization of this book, and thereby have helped to spread Fr. Aloysius's message that Our Blessed Mother is present to each soul in a most intimate way.

About the Author

Fr. Charles Carpenter, M.A.P.: Ordained November 1, 1978; Superior General of the Missionaries of Fatima (1978-2001; 2012-16); Vicar General since 2016. He taught Biblical Theology and Philosophy for fifteen years in the Diocesan Seminary of Ciudad Obregon, Sonora; received a doctorate in Spiritual Theology from the Gregorian University, Rome (1997), with the thesis: *Theology as the Road to Holiness in Saint Bonaventure.*

Photoraphy by: Errol Zimmerman

Contact information

For more information on the order Father Aloysius founded, or to be placed on our newsletter mailing list, or to send donations, please use our Stateside address:

Missionaries of Fatima
Post Office Box 10006
Torrance, CA 90505-0706

Our webpage is:

www.missionariesoffatima.org